BEYOND THE HEADLINES
TRUTHS OF SOWETO LIFE

BEYOND THE HEADLINES
TRUTHS OF SOWETO LIFE

NOMAVENDA MATHIANE

SOUTHERN
BOOK PUBLISHERS

ISBN 1 86812 300 6

First edition, first impression 1990

Published by
Southern Book Publishers (Pty) Ltd
PO Box 548, Bergvlei 2012
Johannesburg

Set in 10½ on 11½ pt Andover
by Unifoto, Cape Town
Printed and bound by Sigma Press, Pretoria

Contents

Foreword

F OR a lady with a large number of firmly held opinions, Nomavenda Mathiane has very few enemies.

Part of the reason is personality. She is perpetually bouyant. Make that BOUYANT. There is a wry grin and a long slow wink. Her body language is an artwork: just a little lift of the eyebrows and a little drawing-down of the corner of the mouth. She can put several different expressions into the twitch of a cheek muscle. You don't need to wait for her to reply to your argument. By the time you've finished stating it you're beginning to doubt it yourself.

The rest of the reason is honesty. Noma says the most scandalous things. She says them all the time. She grabs your sacred cow by the horns. She tramps on its toes; she wrings its neck; she pushes it through a mangle. Then she sweetly offers you the remains. Normally, you'd take up arms, but when it's coming from Noma you know that it's nothing personal. She is giving everybody else's sacred cows the same treatment. Which mitigates the damage somewhat.

This makes Nomavenda unconventional. She'd be unconventional anywhere, I suppose, but in South Africa things often tend to be a little sharper than in a lot of other places. Here, orthodoxies do not merely prevail; they have us pinned to the ground. It is unheard of for people to question *everybody*. You are meant to have heroes, and to avert your gaze from the feet of clay.

Nor is it exactly common for people to talk straight and keep friends. On the black side of the great divide, it is the worst. Most of the various warring militant and quasi-militant movements have a very straightforward view: either you are ours or you are the enemy.

Well, Nomavenda is in a class of her own. She'll say out loud the things everybody else only mumbles quietly among consenting adults in private. And she still has friends.

I met Nomavenda late in 1976. A friend had brought her to my house, and I looked upon her with great suspicion.

At that time I was in a position of perpetual distrust, like a prison cook or an army quartermaster.

I was working at *World*, a black newspaper that had suddenly become a cult after the uprising of June that year. Everybody wanted to work at *World*. It was all of a sudden "relevant". Those of us left over from the pre-fashionable days became cynical. We drowned in sycophancy. There was always a hidden agenda. We were used to being told how wonderful *World* was, as a prelude to an enquiry about staff openings.

The subject of *World* duly came up. Nomavenda hadn't known I worked there. Finding out, she gave me an earful: that *World* was second-rate; that it was a sham, a so-called black paper largely run by whites; and much more, blunt and fierce.

Well, *World* needed nothing so much as an antidote to the flood of head-swelling, and I wanted Noma there. I finally talked her into it. She became my secretary.

She was a terrible secretary, entirely lacking in a sense of due care and responsibility towards my lunch dates, my phone messages and my filing system.

But she wanted to write. She wasn't trained or qualified as a journalist, but she wanted to write. She pounded at her ancient manual typewriter, exploring, experimenting. Her copy was not great. Hardly any was used. But she was looking for something; the truth as she saw it and not as she was meant to see it.

Then *World* was banned. Its phoenix arose a week later, under the name *Post*, but Noma and I were sacked. The end, I thought, of an interesting incipient journalistic career.

But the finger of fate is not to be prescribed to. There was a small new Black Consciousness paper called *The Voice*. Unlike the established papers, it wasn't strong on degrees and track records of potential writers. The criteria were simple — be black, be proud, spell recognisably, deliver.

Suddenly, Nomavenda was no longer a secretary with aspirations. She was a journalist. More than that, a columnist. Instant status.

Noma had always known about half the population of Soweto — if you're planning to walk two blocks with her, budget 40 minutes to allow for greetings. In the *Voice* era she got to know the other half.

But the *Voice* era was brief. *The Voice* made various forms of legal history, one of them when an edition was banned for, among other things, referring to the censors as censors. You were meant to call them "publications controllers". Finally it died, not so much a victim of the State as suffocated by the overkindness of its benefactors.

Still, Nomavenda was a journalist now. There were places to go.

She went, I went, we overlapped here and there. In 1986 we got together at a small magazine, comprised of us two — since joined by another.

What we are doing here, we often wonder. For me, one of the redeeming features is what Nomavenda writes. I look at her copy and think: "Who the hell else would have the guts to say that?"

DENIS BECKETT

Preface

QUITE often when writers read some of their old stuff, they want to bury their heads in shame. In some cases one becomes astonished at the level of growth, understanding and development reflected in one's writing.

Yet when I went through what I wrote last year, I found my whole body shaking when reading about the year 1986, which to me was the bloodiest year of my life. The year when South Africa's black areas seemed to be engulfed in a black cloud. From Uitenhage to Nelspruit, Durban to Duduza, smoke billowed up in the sky, gunshots pierced the midnight tranquillity and mothers' screams tore through the day. A year when black students fought it out at bus-stops and football grounds; where brother killed brother; where even 11-year-olds were seen as too dangerous to be left to roam the streets.

"It is not enough that they have taken our husbands and sons away from us, now they have taken our grandchildren," said Mrs Urbania Mothopeng.

That was the year when for the first time in my life I envied whites in their cocooned and safe, comfortable homes. The year where I would walk into the office, look at Denis Beckett and before I could open my mouth he would say "bhala" (write). The year when everybody was immobilised, when we wished we could wake up from this terrible nightmare.

Tombstones would sprout in township cemeteries countrywide, houses were rebuilt elsewhere, while in some places, ruins of what used to be homes remained testimony to the struggle.

And as I write, all is quiet. Many say it's a lull before the storm. I pray not. Lord don't let it happen again.

At this stage, I would like to thank Denis Beckett, editor of *Frontline*, who made this book possible by insisting that I "bhala" all that I was going through. At times I'd think he was enjoying my discomfort, the pain of replaying tapes I would have preferred to forget. It was not pleasant having to rewrite some incidents I'd prayed never to re-experience, ever. He made me write it all.

Lastly, thanks to my children who never understood my strange behaviour. How could they understand that I was helplessly witnessing a nation disintegrate. And my brothers and sisters for unending love.

NOMAVENDA MATHIANE

1

The gathering tragedy

TWENTY schools have already been officially closed and more are surely to follow. It looks as though yet another year has been wasted.

At the beginning of August, Soweto students called for a school stayaway in protest at the presence of the South African Defence Force in schools. Their demands included the release of detained political prisoners and school colleagues hurled into jail during the state of emergency.

Until the government meets their demands, they have decided to go to school for two days a week — Mondays and Tuesdays. The rest of the week they loiter in the townships.

Last year, all seemed normal until September when students started calling for the postponement of the final-year examinations. Affected most were final-year matric students.

The Government was bent on going ahead with the examinations while militant students threatened to assault whoever sat for the exams. The result? A few students tried to write, but they were about to be lynched by other students. They had to abandon the idea.

Others sought to write at some privately set up venues. But for most students, a year had been wasted.

At the beginning of this year there was mayhem as students flocked back to school demanding, in some instances, to be pushed to the next class. Using the slogan "an injury to one is an injury to all," schoolyard logic demanded "pass one, pass all". Some had not seen the inside of a classroom for years.

They wrote examinations sometime around Easter and, of course, demanded to be promoted.

As things stand in Soweto and most townships, schooling has long ceased to be an educational matter. It is political.

Since 1976 when the students protested against the use of Afrikaans and thousands of people got killed, the education of the black child has moved from the parents and educationists into the political arena.

The tragedy of this situation is that, in view of the prevailing political climate, the more fortunate black parents have removed their children from trouble-torn schools and have either taken them to the homelands or to white schools. Those children left behind who wish to go to school cannot, and woe unto those who dare go against "the will of the people".

The result is a new division in black society. Ordinary parents, for instance, feel great resentment towards those upper class politicos with children at posh schools in the Northern Suburbs.

Then there are those "leaders" whose children study abroad while daddy stays home "fanning the fires of the struggle" — the same fires which keep the children of most township blacks illiterate and out of school.

And then there are the activists who have been planning to call back children who are at boarding schools and at white schools. In fact, threats have been made to children attending white schools that their school combis will be set alight.

Another tragedy is that of Soweto itself. Its very size makes it uncontrollable. In some townships life and schools are relatively normal, while in other areas going to school has become a thing of the past. There is no way, for instance, a child can hope to attend school normally in townships like Diepkloof and Meadowlands — already aptly dubbed "Beirut".

Added to that, communication between students of various townships is rather difficult. Recently a 13-year-old girl travelling by train to school was assaulted by "comrades" who asked her if she didn't know that it was meant to be a stayaway day.

There is talk of students calling for "People's Education". Propagators of this type of education claim black students are being taught distorted history and that the education fails to prepare the children for the adult world.

To many South African parents, that is old hat. In fact, a lot was said and written about this when Bantu education was introduced in the fifties. Came the 1976 black student uprisings and once again the inferiority of the black education system was under the spotlight.

So far, nobody has explained to an average black parent what is meant by this People's Education. They need to know whether it is an ideology, a concept, a document or a syllabus. They want to know if today, in 1986, there is machinery ready to put it into action. They want to know if it is an alternative to the present system of education, or "brainwashing", or a gimmick, or a temporary tactic of a faction in the struggle, or does it offer real hope. Presently there are three schools of thought vis-à-vis black education . . .

The first calls for "liberation now and education later". The second calls for People's Education. Both of these schools seem to be aligned with existing political movements.

The third school is the school of ordinary "non-political" people, who feel a black child is being made a sacrificial lamb.

Since the political movements are known to be active in all areas, why is it that it is only the Soweto child who is expected to boycott school. Schooling is normal in Eldorado and in Lenasia. What will happen when uhuru comes?

Black South Africans tend to want to draw a parallel with the Zimbabwe experience. Indeed, Zimbabwe is a shining example of what may be achieved. But, the Zimbabwe kids who became disenchanted with the old system went to the bush. When the battle was won, Mugabe was able to absorb the guerillas into the army.

What will happen to the black youth who has neither been to school nor to the bush? Who is even thinking about this Frankenstein monster, this typical Soweto teenager, who is presently ravaging the townships?

When Samora Machel in Mozambique won the war, he was faced by a nation where four in every five members of the population were illiterate. One of his first priorities was to change that. In fact, the whole of Africa has been fighting against illiteracy.

In South Africa the black education gap was beginning to narrow. Never mind that for years people have been screaming that the education is inferior to that of the whites.

The fact of the matter is, inferior as it is, the blacks who took advantage of it have not burnt their certificates and folded their arms in despair. Nor do we see them as generals of the "liberation-now-and-education-later" infantry.

Instead, they have carried their heads high, used black education as a launching pad to acquire more. We have them as doctors, lawyers and scientists — both inside and outside the country.

Meanwhile, the war rages on in the schools. Even if the Government does not close the schools down, there is no way that students in Soweto will sit for the end-of-year examinations. Even if they did, on what will they be tested? What can they have absorbed in their two-day school week? Another year has been lost. And, as the struggle continues, they are growing older. They have to be admitted at universities or find work. Where will the "pass-one, pass-all" tactic lead?

Unfortunately the situation in Soweto is such that people live in fear. There is a strongly believed myth that the students are a faceless and leaderless mob and nobody dares question their actions.

The leader who survives these days is the one who endorses whatever the youth says, be it wrong or right. People have opted for popularity with the students because opposing them is to invite being "necklaced".

Another disturbing dimension is the quiet stand seen to be taken by the ANC as well as the PAC in this regard. The education delegation which met the ANC in Harare earlier this year reported back that the ANC wants the students back into class. But it would seem that message was not broadcast loud enough.

Parents feel there ought to be a stronger call from the movement for the children to go back to school. The parents feel that somehow students are under the impression that the ANC condones their actions. They are of the opinion that if the ANC could condemn the non-schooling of kids maybe the children would see the rationale behind schooling and they might just go back.

But there is another argument advanced — that there is no way the ANC could condemn non-schooling because children are in actual fact doing what the ANC is not doing — fighting the SA government. But those in touch with reality know that it is not possible for children throwing stones to bring down the government. They see these children as sitting ducks for the SADF troops.

So, if the students go back to class who will then fight the liberation war? And there lies the rub.

Any well-meaning organisation will not unnecessarily expose the wider society, let alone its youth, to danger. Monkeys, when attacked, the older ones form a laager around the young ones for protection and preservation of their kind.

Everybody knows the value of education. And if it was in the nation's interest to withdraw children from school, parents would oblige. But it is national suicide to deny youth education, hence the divisions and killings we're experiencing.

2

Diary of troubled times

———————— NOVEMBER 1986 ————————

TUESDAY night, 26 August: I am seated in my living room helping my 14-year-old daughter with her homework. The phone rings. It is my elder sister who lives in Rockville.

I knew immediately that something was wrong. She is not the type to phone for nothing. She is a very calm person by nature. In fact, she is the one who is always in control in my family when things go wrong.

I remember when my father died, I performed, screaming and throwing myself on the floor. My brother held me and tried to calm me down. Nothing could help. As if possessed by spirits, I continued crying.

Anyway, it was my sister Catherine who simply said, "Look, it's Monday today and the old man will only be buried on Saturday. Don't you think you had better save the energy for then?"

That did the trick. I sobered up. If this will help you understand her nature better, then I should also add that she is a nursing sister. Tough.

So when I heard her voice on the line I knew something had happened. One of my sisters? My brother perhaps? Or could it be the old girl? (my eighty-year-old mother who hardly ever gets sick). I held my breath.

"Carol, I don't know what is happening. We are hearing so much shooting and I believe people in White City are being evicted."

"What, why should they evict people at night?" was my first reaction.

My daughter closed her book and, with eyes about to fall out their sockets, looked at me, obviously trying to follow the conversation.

My sister told me that she had just returned from the "street committee meeting" where it was decided they keep their lights on at both front and back, and to respond to any neighbour blowing a whistle asking for help.

"There is so much shooting, I wonder if there will still be people alive tomorrow."

She thought it was about rents, which is a nightmare. If you pay, you can get the necklace. So nobody pays, but people are scared of being evicted, or of one day, when all this is over, having to pay months and months of back rent.

"There was also another problem: Two boys from my area have been stabbed to death.

"Apparently a gang went to a shebeen, held up the owner and got away with some cash. When they had to share the money, they quarrelled and one took out a knife and killed the two. Do you know what this means?

"The families that have lost their sons might want to burn this boy's home and the shebeen owner is not going to take kindly to what these boys did to him.

"Where will all this end? Is it fair that we should be dragged in this mess? I mean, I don't know the inside of a shebeen, but when houses burn I might just get dragged in it. Is it fair?"

I tried to pacify her and tell her that things will get right. Nothing was going to happen to her. (But I was not sure.) I wondered if I would speak to her again.

We held on to the phone not saying anything. I could hear her breathing on the other end of the line as we had gone beyond the mmm's and the ahhh's. She hung up. In the meantime, shooting was continuing. I now had to attend to my girl who had a barrage of questions.

"Will the soldiers come to Chiawelo too?

"Why do they have to shoot?

"Are people resisting evictions?

"How long are we going to stay without paying rent?

"Does it make sense to you, Ma, that we should just stay without paying rent?

"Why don't they release Mandela to sort out all this mess?"

I tried as best I could to reassure her that they were not likely to come to our township because our matter was being attended to. That we started boycotting the rent long before it was a national issue because of the unfair amount we are being charged. I don't know whether I was convincing or not as I also needed somebody to reassure me right then. But eventually we called it a night, and I continued my reading in bed.

It first sounded like a firecracker and far away, but, strange enough, I could no longer concentrate on my book. I heard it again and this time I knew it wasn't Guy Fawkes crackers. It was gunshots. I sat up and put the light off. Then there were more gunshots.

I got off the bed, tip-toed into my living room to see what was going on. I peeped through the curtains and there was not a soul in sight. Then the dogs started barking. From all yards, dogs barked and the sound of gunfire was deafening.

I went into my other child's bedroom. She was sitting on her bed, eyes wide open. She asked: "What's going on here?"

I could not answer her. I went into the bathroom and when I came out both my girls were standing in the passage. The younger one asked: "Are they here now, Ma?"

I shook my head. I saw lights go on in my neighbour's house. I went to the phone and dialled. As someone said "hello", there was a sound of a gunshot. I dropped the receiver and ran to my bedroom. The girls said we should go under the bed, but my bed has a base so we couldn't. We huddled on my bed. How I wished there was a man in the house to protect us.

I have always felt my bed was too big. But with two teenage girls and myself on it, it was like a cot.

My little one held on to me and her heart was pounding like a machine. We prayed with our eyes wide open, all of us at the same time. Sleep overcame us.

Next day I knocked off early from work, planning to have an early night. I thought of getting sleeping tablets to knock me out, but settled for a bottle of wine instead. When I got home, I called my sister who informed me her neighbour's son had been found dead from bullet wounds.

As I drew the curtains in preparation to sleep, I saw a neighbour who I have not seen for some time. I ran out the house and we stood chatting about the night before.

Then, as we stood talking, we saw a group of about 8 boys entering yards. I suggested we stand and wait for them as opposed to them finding us in our homes. They told us that the boers were coming to evict us, so we should keep our lights on and doors open front and back so those being chased by soldiers can take refuge. I went back into the house and told the girls that there might just be trouble that night.

We were having supper when the first shot went off. We ran to the living room to see if there were any police cars about or youngsters. The street was deserted. We went back to the kitchen but could only look at the food. We moved to the living room and sat on the floor.

It was getting very dark outside. We saw car lights moving on our street. I prayed that it would be a friend visiting us. But it wasn't. And we continued sitting in silence. Then a shot went off, followed by another, and another one.

I started panicking. I needed someone to help us. I grabbed hold of the phone. I wanted to phone my brother to come and fetch us. But I realised there was no way he could drive past bullets and get here. I thought maybe phoning him and letting him know that we were in trouble would make me feel better. His line was engaged. Dare I scare my sister? I decided against it and suddenly wanted to speak to someone who wasn't caught up in the mess. I phoned a colleague, in the suburbs on the other side of town.

It was as though he had been waiting for my call. My voice could not come out. When it did, I told him there was lots of shooting and we were scared. He asked pertinent questions and ended by asking what was I going to do and what could he do. I screamed "Nothing".

At that stage I was shaking like a leaf. I let the receiver face the street so that he could hear the sounds of gunfire. He mumbled something I could not hear. I hung up while he was talking. I ran to my bedroom and changed into my pyjamas. My girls, realising the state I was in, started giggling. I suspect it was a reaction. In their shocked state it was a relief to laugh at mother making herself ridiculous. I knew they were equally scared.

Then the phone rang. I started. I was too scared to walk to the living room where the phone was. I feared someone might see me walk in the passage and shoot me. I crawled to the phone. Then my pyjamas caught on the carpet and I fell on my face. And the phone kept ringing while the girls laughed. Outside the shooting continued.

I reached the phone after many seconds which felt like many days. It was the friend I had called earlier. I told him not to worry and that I would phone him if and when I needed help. I hung up. I hoped he had got the message not to phone me. As I was about to crawl back to my bedroom, the phone went on again. "What is it?" I snapped. It was a friend from Cape Town. He wanted to know if we were safe. I told him there was trouble and he promised to pray for me and the kids. I thanked him and hung up.

One of the girls told me to tell my friends not to phone us. Strangely enough she had also crawled to where I was.

Shooting was still going on outside as we crawled back to the bedroom. It now sounded as though they were shooting on the next street. We sat on my bedroom floor, holding each other's hands. My big girl suggested that we stand against the wall next to the window so that if anyone shot through the windows the bullets wouldn't touch us. It sounded a brilliant idea. I asked her where she got it from. She quoted the "A-Team". I gave up.

Dogs continued barking. Then we heard footsteps in the yard and something fall. I closed Bongi's mouth just before she could scream and we waited. We discovered the next morning that it was a huge dog scavenging in my refuse bin. We went on our knees like we do in church, prayed and slept.

We woke up to a normal day with newspaper headlines of trouble in Soweto. I could barely walk. Sharing a bed with two other people is most uncomfortable and, added to that, carrying tension for two nights just about crippled me. I thought of phoning my boss to tell him that I could not make it, but realised if I stayed home I would probably have to deal with the soldiers.

Work was a form of escapism. Even if for only 11 hours. I dragged myself to the bus-stop.

In the taxi, everybody was talking about the shooting. Their personal experiences and some of their relatives' and friends' were recounted. One woman told how her aunt had slept on top of her son, hiding him from the soldiers. The narrator was very dramatic and had the taxi in stitches as she drew the picture of her big-bosomed aunt squashing the poor boy beneath her. We drove past many Casspirs . . . and ambulances.

One of my friends came to the office. She was livid with rage.

"You know what my son has done? He has put us into trouble. The comrades came to tell him to join them. They did not find him and they left a strong message that he should join them or else they will set our home on fire. When he got back he refused to go. He said he was not prepared to be shot for nothing. Do you know what this means? They will burn our house because of him."

I tried to tell her: "What do you expect the child to do? He is afraid. Don't you understand?"

She didn't.

"Look, I am also afraid, but he has to go. He is a sissy. He must just go. Otherwise we will all die."

In the afternoon, my brother phoned to say our younger brother's wife had been mugged and was in bad shape. He offered to take me to see her. I asked my boss if I could knock off early as I was not feeling too good.

Frankly, I did not have the heart to tell him where I was going. I just thought some things are better not told, especially as there was no logic in mugging a poor woman on her way to work. Mugging someone when the heat was so much on for more important matters. I mean, how does one explain that behaviour?

I called home and told them I would be late as "uncle and I had to go somewhere". They told me to be careful. I assured them that I would not fall.

Apparently they have been entertaining people with stories of how I fell over my pyjamas in my panic and that I may seem tough on the outside, but I was a paw-paw inside.

The weekend was uneventful. Come Monday and I started the day with a call from my friend whose son refused to join the comrades. Now the comrades want to burn her. She told me the comrades had once more come looking for her son and when she objected to their manner of approach they got angry and said they were going to necklace her.

"Do you actually think they will do it?"

What could I say to that? How do I know the behaviour of people who necklace other people? Is there a pattern one could perhaps follow or read about to explain the thinking of such people?

She was very worried.

"I mean, all I am guilty of is asking these kids why did they have to be so rude when knocking on my door. They knocked as though we were harbouring criminals. Knocking at every door and shining torches all over. Now I am to be necklaced."

I suggested that she should move in with me. "I have thought of that, but then they will think I am scared of them. No, I am not going anywhere. Let them do whatever they want." (So far nothing has happened to her. Touch wood.)

In the meantime, there was mounting talk of the mass funeral to be held on Thursday. Rumour had it everybody had to attend the funeral. In the meantime, the Minister of Law and Order (What law? As for order, the less said, the better) has already banned the funerals. We were once more heading for what may be a fatal confrontation.

The next day I am told there is talk about an indefinite stayaway from school, to go un until the troops leave the townships and release detained students. A friend calls me to a meeting for parents to give their views.

The meeting is attended mainly by women and students. The women are angry.

"I don't understand your logic," says one woman. "The boers are closing down the schools and you are calling a boycott. In whose interest is all this? The boers do not care a damn if you go to school or not and you are playing right into their hands."

10

The meeting gets out of order as it become obvious that there is no way the children will listen.

One of the students goes on a long talk about how the parents have not taken any interest in their kids. "We have had enough. Try and read under the barrel of a gun. We are not wanting too much by wanting the SADF out the schoolyards.

"In fact, you mothers actually surprise me. If the white women were faced with the same problem they would have picked up their skirts and fought the army out of their locations. These people are there to kill us."

It is a hopeless situation. In one corner of us, we (the mothers) admire those children and how determined they are. But we did not want liberation to be like this. The meeting went on with no more word about the adults' concerns.

The children called the tune and our only role was to sit and listen, in angry silence. It was not even as if they were a majority. They were a handful.

Wednesday found everybody worried about the next day (the day of the funeral). I knocked off early, anticipating transport problems. We had an early supper. Knowing we were not going to work the next day, we indulged in watching a movie on television.

Around 10, a car stopped outside. We turned the lights off and peeped through the window. It was a friend. We let him in. He joined us, watched the movie and the little girl soon retired to sleep.

In between watching we spoke about the funeral and what was likely to happen. I kept teasing him that as an ex-political prisoner he was meant to know what was going on. He told me that people of his generation were regarded as "hasbeens" and the young radicals had taken over and "that lot does not listen to anybody's advice".

We were seated in that semi-darkness talking and watching the movie when suddenly dogs started barking. Soon there were whistles and voices. I stopped breathing for a second. I rushed to the window and looked through the curtains.

A group of young boys and girls were throwing stones at my neighbour's house. I knew what it was. The next house would be mine. It is comrades collecting girls to attend the funeral vigil.

"Open up," I heard the youngsters call. At that stage I was shaking like a leaf. Then I saw shadows move towards my house. I collected my nerves and told my friend to open for them at the kitchen door and ask them to wait while he wakes me up.

I remembered that a little while earlier we had bought a new cupboard. Bongi gave it one look and said, in what I thought was jest: "Now I know where I will hide when comrades come looking for me."

11

I bet her she couldn't fit, and in fun she got in to prove her point.

That piece of childish fun was in my mind as I ran to my bedroom where Bongi was fast asleep. I rudely shook her. She did not wake up. I couldn't carry her so I dragged her to the cupboard and locked her in. I then quickly took my dress off and threw my robe on as though I had just come out of bed. I met my friend at my bedroom door. He was accompanied by three boys.

The youths said they wanted my daughter. I looked them straight in the eyes and told them she was visiting my sister. I then walked past them to the door in a gesture to show them out. There were, I found, more youths in my yard. If they did not believe my story, they did not show it as they milled out.

They moved to the next house where there is a teenage girl and boy. I went back into the house and ran to release Bongi before she suffocated. She walked half awake back to bed.

I peeped through the window and could see the youngsters moving into another house. Suddenly, I was gripped by another fear. What if they should decide to hijack my friend's car to the vigil?

"I think you must go," I heard myself say.

He suddenly became furious. "Why do I have to be dictated to by children! I will go when I want to. Besides, I have the papers to my car so there is no way they can say my car is a target."

It took quite a while to convince him that once they decided they wanted his car there was very little he could do to stop them. Besides, if they went away with the feeling that I was associating with people who refuse to transport them, then I might be in trouble.

Having convinced him of the wisdom of leaving, I also asked him to take my daughter away with him in case they came back to search the house. Again, he didn't feel comfortable with the thought of leaving me alone. Ultimately, reason prevailed and we bundled Bongi in the car and they drove off.

Alone, I had a good opportunity to work myself into a state. I was now too scared to even go to my bedroom. I put all the lights out — comrades' orders or not — and took the scatter pillows and placed them on the floor.

I thought of phoning my brother and decided against it. What was the point of waking the poor chap, especially now Bongi was away and safe? I dialled my boss. We spoke in low tones. There was no light in the house except for the two bars of the heater. He suggested I get sleeping tablets. I told him I had none. He said I should get brandy. We both chuckled because he knows I never get beyond wine.

He sounded more worried than I. I was now sorry for having rung him. I thought of dawn. The creaking of the asbestos roof, something that happens every day, sounded like someone throwing things on the roof. I do not know when sleep overcame me, but I remember waking up feeling cold and stiff.

Outside was a bright September morning. But already people were standing in groups outside yards looking at the main road where a contingent of army cars was moving towards Regina Mundi.

The day drags on with all sorts of rumours circling the townships. There are not many cars moving about. I walk to the main road where I find one taxi fellow being told to off-load passengers as no taxi is allowed to operate that day. People get off and start walking. One of them is a nurse coming from doing night duty in town.

Around Regina Mundi, a group of soldiers are standing in the church-grounds while some are parked outside the yard. I notice some more army trucks parked in the recreation park at Rockville. I meet a colleague who is making rounds of the townships. I join him in the car. We drive to the cemetery (Avalon) where we find soldiers guarding the main entrance. It is quite obvious there is not going to be any burial.

On our way home we notice a group of people going round the back entrance. We have no doubt they mean to bury their dead. At that stage the army helicopters dominate the sky as they fly this way and that. We leave the uncertain situation at the cemetery and go to the stadium. There is nobody there and the mood of the people around Soweto is angry. They cannot understand why they are prevented from burying their dead. I go home.

Friday comes and goes without much happening. Everywhere people speak of the highhandedness of the law. In the taxi to work people are talking about the rowdiness and uncontrollable state of the youth. One woman was agitated by the government for its refusal to release Mandela.

"All what these childen want to see is Mandela. I think he can put an end to all this tyranny."

Another was quick to say "Why don't they just grab any old man and parade him before the kids as Mandela — the blighters don't know him after all."

The discussions centred around the youth and the soldiers. Everybody wanted something to be done to redress the situation. Everybody was crying for security and a return to a normal life: a life where people can bury their dead peacefully, where children can go to school and not be intimidated by the presence of soldiers in their school premises, where neighbours can feel free with each other and where children can roam the streets as children, not as comrades.

I don't usually wake up early on Saturday mornings. It was about

8.30 am and I had just drunk my first cup of coffee. From my kitchen door I caught sight of a boy running towards me.

He bursts in through the kitchen door, runs into one of the bedrooms and tries to hide beneath a bed. I run after him and ask "What do you want?"

All the child could say was: "It's bad. The boers are here."

He dives into the blankets, clothes and all. I tell him how stupid it is of him to sleep with his clothes on. Who would believe him, whatever story he had. He gets the message, undresses and throws his clothes at me.

I lock them in the wardrobe and find half full bottles of old medicines and place them on the floor next to the bed. All this happens in less than five minutes.

Outside I hear gumboot steps in the yard. I know the soldiers are here looking for him. I quickly move into the toilet. I hear them struggle with my kitchen door. One thing about my kitchen door is that it opens from outside. So you could be out there pushing when all you need to do is pull. No amount of complaining to the West Rand board could persuade them to fix the door.

Ultimately, the soldiers got the door right. I heard them walk in the kitchen, I flushed the toilet and came out. Rifles were pointing at me. They seemed more surprised than I was. I don't know what they expected to see.

It was quiet in the room. My cat crept closer to my feet as the soldiers walked to my living room, looked around, opened one bedroom door after another. I held my breath. They moved into the bedroom where my supposed patient was sleeping — and left him to sleep.

Outside, more soldiers were scouting the area. Some were in the next yard and people stood outside watching. The ones in my house walked out. I started sweeping my yard so as to be in touch with what was going on outside.

Having exhausted their search in my street, the soldiers moved to the next one.

I gave the boy an old shirt that had been lying around for some time. Having eaten the sandwich I had prepared, he thanked me profusely.

But there was no way I could not have saved that child. To me, it was not an issue for debate. It had nothing to do with principle or morality. He was a child who had to be hid or killed. I didn't wait to ask him why he was involved or not involved. At the same time, I saw in my mind's eye a group of boys taking somebody's car. He could be one of those youths who are merciless when they

14

want their way. He could have been one of those who came for my daughter. He could have been one of those who wanted my sister's car or he could be one of those who petrol bomb houses. How was I to know? What would you have done?

I have seen a mother in grief. I have seen a mother coming out of Pretoria Maximum prison after a visit to a son to hang the next day. I have seen a mother watching a corpse of her són covered in papers, waiting for the black maria to remove the body. I have seen a mother escorting a seven-year-old girl to hospital after the child had been raped by a man old enough to be her father. I have seen all that pain and I live with those memories I cannot erase.

Not so many months ago, a colleague asked me how I felt about necklaces. Proudly, I said they were the right treatment for sell-outs, all those people who collaborate with the system.

I remember standing with one hand on my hip and carrying on about just how we (the blacks) are weeding all the bad elements retarding our struggle. He looked at me with a sad face, and I went on talking about the killing by soldiers of three-year-olds playing in the yards.

"Is it fair?" I asked. Why didn't the whites condemn that as much as they condemn necklaces. I was convinced we were on the right track.

One afternoon three weeks later I was busy in my house typing away. My daughter burst in. I didn't like the look in her face. She stood there, her face losing colour.

I asked where her friend was. She told me she was at home. I went over and found her in bed. An irate mother said "You know these kids can really make one mad. They go about the streets and look now, they are scared out of their wits. They have just seen a person being necklaced. If they had been at their homes they would not have witnessed such a terrible thing."

So, that's what it was, I said to myself, I went back home, took my child in my arms and told her it would be over one day. We sat down and cried.

I decided to go back to my typing but couldn't.

Something said I should go and see that necklace victim, but I was too scared. Eventually, the journalist in me got the better of me and I went out amid protests from my daughter.

I made a few enquiries and people pointed the way the victim and mob went. A young boy ran past. His face had gone a strange grey colour.

I was about to turn back when I saw a group of people. Some were seated, others standing. I wanted to turn back but realised that I might get into trouble and be asked why was I making a U-turn.

15

I met some women in the way, talking in loud voices, condemning the killing.

"Poor child," one woman said. "What has he done?" I asked.

They shrugged their shoulders and I went ahead.

I didn't actually see the victim. His charred remains were by then covered in papers and pieces of plastic. I saw the mother. She was crying, without tears coming out. If maybe you have seen a sangoma dance in a trance maybe you will begin to understand.

She was crying and talking all the time. Maybe she was in a state of shock. But she was mumbling that her child is not a witch, but is sick. And she was crying to her God in Shangaan or Venda. She looked at us without seeing us. We looked at each other. There were women mostly (it was during the week) and a few policemen around. No-one except the mother said anything. We just looked on.

People came, looked, got tired and left. It must have been sometime in the evening when the body was removed. Another victim of the struggle. Another day in Soweto.

3

The strange, strange feeling of taking control

THE sight of a group of boys calling house to house has become common. It is unnerving. You think "for whom does the bell toll?" When a group came up to my door and told me to attend a meeting the next night to form a street committee for my street I was at first apprehensive. But the boys were polite.

I began to see an opportunity for me and my neighbours to organise ourselves so we would not be alone and at the mercy of the comrades. It seemed ironic that it was the comrades themselves who were inspiring this, but I started to get interested.

The meeting was to be held at a friend's place. I went to sound her out on the meeting. Apparently her house had been chosen because it had recently been enlarged.

I found her terribly agitated. She could not understand why she should be picked on when she was a woman staying alone with her children.

"There are so many men staying in this street, why is the meeting not held in a man's house?"

I told her as far as I was concerned, that was not an issue to waste time on. What I thought important was the opportunity to get together as people of that street, get to know each other, and, above all, form strategies to solve our problems as a people.

I am not sure if she agreed with me or not, but when the evening came, my neighbours and myself started converging to her house. At first people walked in, looked at each other suspiciously, greeted and sat down.

I really do not know what we were expecting. Of course, there were fears that the police might come in and detain the whole lot of us. Worse still, they could just get there and open fire. But then, so many people have died lately that one feels the presence of death all the time. And above that, we have heard stories about other townships neighbours getting together and sorting out unruly elements.

One by one, people started coming in. It had been raining the whole week, so the night appeared to be blacker than it should have been, adding a sinister note to an already pregnant evening.

The convenors (comrades) arrived and were also given the suspicious and apprehensive looks. There were only three boys, not older than 18. As they stood addressing us, they shuffled their feet and rubbed their hands (I think they were nervous).

They introduced themselves. I am not sure those were their real names. They gave us the reasons for wanting to form a street committee. They said we need to protect ourselves, first from the boers who want to evict us from our houses; we also need to protect ourselves against com-tsotsis (these are thugs who masquerade as comrades). But more than that, they said, they wanted to be together with us as parents.

Then the meeting was open to the people. Like a pack of wolves, the parents descended on the three boys. "Where do you come from?" "Where will you take our names to?" "Where is your headquarters?" "Do your parents know you are here?" were some of the questions being asked, and all at the same time.

We were about to have a nasty confrontation when one man spoke: "It's not as if you people do not know that street committees are being formed in most parts of Soweto. In this street we have had comrades coming here demanding our children, girls especially, to go to funeral vigils.

"The formation of a street committee is going to give us power to do what action we want to take and not have them tell us adults what to do."

That did the trick. Some women were obviously still angry. Understandably, too. For there they were face to face with people who were harassing them and making life impossible.

It was obvious they had come along to give the boys a good telling-off and to say "to hell with the street committee".

The boys were humble. First, they confessed they were not familiar with the jargon used at meetings, let alone conversant with procedures.

Some women offered to open a night school for them. "Ma, we are boycotting schools." That derailed the meeting as questions such

18

as "what do you hope to be without education?" were thrown at the boys.

Someone realised that we were now off at a tangent and protested: "We are not here to discuss the school crisis."

The people got back to the purpose of the meeting.

Gradually the ice began to thaw as the boys explained their stand and what we had to do.

People asked for clarification on matters such as "does it mean if you want to tell us anything you will go to our chairman who will call a meeting and communicate to us your problem?"

They agreed.

"Does this mean you won't come knocking at out door demanding our children?"

The answer to that was: girls were no longer to be taken away at night. Parents heaved a sigh of relief.

The boys went on to explain how some elements were masquerading as comrades. The street committee would work closely with the comrades and fight all the unwanted elements.

They also told us no cars would be hijacked and Putco buses were no longer to be stoned.

"What is the point of stoning buses driven by our fathers? It is our parents who get killed and not the owners of the buses."

By this time, the parents were interested. We had also ceased to be on the receiving end — just there to receive orders from the boys. We were participating in the running of our affairs — something new in the lives of most of us.

Not only that. We had been gathered as strangers who have lived next door since 1982. Suddenly we were no longer strangers and this feeling was to continue long after the meeting. In fact, we got to know each other better and better.

We then got down to the business of electing the executive. After a great argument with people refusing to stand for elections, giving lame excuses such as "I knock off late from work" or "I am already committed elsewhere," a man over 50 years old, who had made an impression with the sense of his comments during the meeting, was chosen chairman. But not before telling the house that he was accepting on one condition: that he would never have to be told to necklace people or burn down anybody's house.

"I am saying so because our politics are no longer run democratically. If you disagree with the crowd then you get necklaced. If I am called to do that, I want to tell you here and now that I will stop being chairman of this committee."

Once more the comrades reassured him that they would not do

any such thing. In fact, they said they were also against the necklaces and burnings. Our names were taken down as well as those of the executives. We were further told to buy a particular type of whistle, different from the ones used by the blackjack police.

These whistles are to be used when attacked by anybody, whether soldiers, blackjacks or thugs. The idea is to blow the whistle if attacked and, on hearing that, the neighbours come out to your assistance.

Unfortunately, recently in one area, people came out on hearing the sound of the whistle and were shot at.

The executive was also drawn from people who had contributed during the course of the meeting. One of them was a bus driver who has links with a football organisation. It was obvious that his soccer club experience in respect of running meetings would be an asset for our street.

With the executive chosen and business out of the way, we spent some time chatting to the boys and getting to know them. It was amazing the amount of goodwill created within a few minutes. The boys who we had viewed with suspicion and anger had become midwives of security and understanding.

For days after that, I would meet some of my neighbours and we would actually stop and chat. In fact, last week after four people had died in Phomolong, our chairman suggested we look beyond whistles for protection. We have now arranged an extra system using telephones, which most people now have.

Not only that, last Saturday a group of so-called comrades came demanding girls for a vigil.

When they came knocking at my door, I told them that the issue had been dealt with at our meeting, that no girl from this street would be going to a funeral vigil. I must have spent less than ten minutes arguing with them when I was joined by a group of women from my street who told the boys off. Previously we would have been too scared.

4

Back to the primus

COMING back from work I am suddenly struck by the unusual darkness of the township. It takes me back to the sixties when there were few houses lit around Soweto, inviting comments such as "walking through Soweto is like walking through a cemetery" from American boxing coach Curtis Coke.

Anyway, it is 1987 and although it is summer, in most cases by six some people have the TV sets on and some of the rooms are lit. This evening it's all dark except for the "Apollo" high mast lights on the street.

I get home and my daughter breaks the news — we have no lights and water. Damn it! At the same time she produces my electricity bill that was delivered during the day. I must pay R114,00 or else I won't have my electricity reconnected.

My mind stops functioning for a minute. So, I think, the hour has come. I look around my kitchen, almost every container has water. Apparently when the blackjacks came dropping the notes, my neighbour who keeps the keys to my house, opened my house and filled every conceivable container with water. I draw a chair and have a good gulp of water and my mind starts functioning once more. Do I have candles for the night? How do we cook?

Fortunately I still have left over candles bought during the "black Christmas boycott" when we had to light candles in solidarity with people in detention. But what do I do for cooking? I mean it is fashionable to give away items such as gas stoves and primus stoves when we move up the ladder. We never seem to have contingency plans.

21

Thank God it is summer and we don't need heaters and hot water. So the evening was spent using water sparingly and talking to neighbours about steps that need to be taken. People are worried about the food rotting in the fridges. Electrical alarm clocks are not working — it is chaotic.

The next day round about noon I phone home to inquire about the water and electricity, I am told these have not been reconnected yet. It is January and mid-month. I cannot afford a fancy gadget like a gas stove. I buy a primus stove.

Although I am a primus stove generation, somehow I just feel I didn't have to be taken back 20 years. With the fumes and noise it's like living in a hostel. But all the same, I suppose I should be at least grateful for small mercies, I could be in some homeland and be expected to make fire on the floor. By now, the water is in short supply. The toilet has not been flushing. To avoid problems, my daughter and I decide to go to the office and school toilets wherever possible and especially for bowel movements. We are only two at home. A neighbour has seven — what a mess. It is amazing how one can take things such as washing hands for granted. Washing hands before getting out of the toilet is second nature to many people. I must have turned on the tap a hundred times.

Each time after pumping the primus stove, I felt paraffin on my hands and I would rush to the tap. At the same time I couldn't just take a cup from the cupboard and dip in the bucket for water, fearing that everything would smell of paraffin. I would have to buy gloves to wear when pumping the primus stove.

The primus is another story. The damn thing makes so much noise you can hardly converse in the house. As for the paraffin fumes it exudes, I got a terrible headache because it being summer, with mosquitoes around one dare not open the door at night. So we had to spend the night in a house full of paraffin smoke.

Not only that, one cannot regulate the stove's heat. It just goes full blast forever so you cannot produce any fancy stuff from it, not that one cares for that during the week but even good old fashioned pap does not need strong heat. And of course, my daughter would not go anywhere near it crying "I don't know how to operate this contraption" — remember she is a child of the seventies where even where there was no electricity at least people used gas.

A primus means cooking one thing at a time. I cooked the pap first and ages later did the meat. By the time the meat was ready, the pap was cold. Vegetables were out of the question. And during the time I was cooking, I was dying for a cuppa tea. How spoilt can one get. One takes it for granted so much that while cooking you can have the kettle on and boil water for tea. I did not even have a kettle to put on the primus stove. I used a small pot for boiling water but the tea thereof was poison.

My shebeen neighbours were the angriest of us all. Business came to a standstill. In fact it was such fun seeing guys trek to the next township in search of cold beers.

On the third day I ran out of candles. How does one run to a neighbour and loan a candle on such days without appearing a fool? My daughter was beside herself with joy — I had for months been keeping a present of a fancy candle refusing that it be used. She brought it and I had no choice but to light it. It was a disaster. The light was not only faint but it flickered throwing wax all over the show, so much for the prize.

That night, she had pages and pages of homework and I told her most doctors and learned people she read about from black areas got their education under candlelight — some from remote areas lit a piece of reed.

We survived the night, as well as the weekend. The water we got back before the weekend, and I must say it was in a way great fun spending a weekend without noise coming from neighbours who own powerful music machines and force people to share their terrible music. It was also interesting to see men not rushing to their next-door shebeen and sort of saunter around the yard complaining about the mess the "comrades" have put them into.

Come Sunday a meeting is called. Everybody turns up. Nothing comes out of it as it is obvious that not much thought has been given over the issues. Questions are asked and it is decided a delegation be sent to the office to find out:

(a) why had the officials chosen to single out this township and punish it by cutting off such services?

(b) how were the meters (especially the water meters) read because there had been no clerks going about reading meter boxes in yards?

(c) what criterion had been used on the electricity bills as the amounts differed between R64 to R900?

The delegation came back a few days later with the news that the officials were not interested in their long story. All they wanted were the tenants to pay and this they were prepared to accept in instalments. The delegates then suggested that people start paying. Trouble began. Delegates were almost assaulted. The reasons advanced were, they were not given a mandate to say the people want to pay and until the whole rent issue is resolved tenants are not prepared to pay.

That divided the house. Some people felt they should compromise.

They should not expect to get services free. Others felt that would be tantamount to giving in and they are not about to do that. Not while the rent issue in the Vaal, where it all started, still has not been resolved. Why does the government not deal with the Vaal first? Others felt once Chiawello Extension 3 pays then they will have let the whole of Soweto down and next time they (Chiawello) are in trouble, greater Soweto will not come to their aid.

Finally, the people agreed to refuse to pay. A few days later, I was surprised to find lights in the windows once again as I walked home. The electricity was back. I was pleased, but in a corner of my mind I wondered: "What next?"

The mood of the people is towards a settlement. Some have come round with suggestions of opening a special savings account where money could be deposited for both rent and services. Their argument is what happens to old people or those who fall under the low income group who do not have large sums of ready cash, when they are suddenly told to pay up? These are the type of people who might be the first victims of evictions. In the meantime, the comrades continue to talk very loud about necklaces, and there is still much fear even though actual cases of necklacing are now few and far between.

About two weeks later, the electricity was cut off again. The chairman of our street committee then visited the office. Finding no answers from the token black superintendents, he finally got through to an especially notorious white superintendent who said he should collect money from the residents to enable them to reconnect the electricity.

This, he was told, was to avoid letting the technicians come out to open up the power boxes for individual houses. It was much easier if it was done en bloc. People thought that was a reasonable offer. And, it also proved that the superintendent was at least prepared to talk to the street committee through its representative.

Having collected the reconnection fee from each house, the chairman went to the office where he found the superintendent had changed his mind. The superintendent would not take the money and instead told the chairman to tell the people to come and see him as individuals. He wanted to make them sign contracts binding them to pay the arrears.

So one by one the people went and paid and we saw lights turning on first in one house then in more. Despite our own anxiety to have our electricity back, many of us were angry to see people scabbing on the boycott. It goes against one's principles.

Also we thought we would see fires or petrol bombs at these houses soon, and maybe the appearance of the necklace. In fact only one person I know of has been necklaced for paying up, and so far only one house in my street has been petrol bombed. But the people who paid are still worried. They feel that their names have been noted.

Anyhow the joke is on them, because now everybody's electricity is off again, whether you paid or not.

When the comrades saw that the people were dividing, it seems that they felt they were losing control. They went with hacksaws to the power boxes and they reconnected everybody.

The whole street had been lighted for three days when the superintendent got wind. Technicians came and switched off the main plant, cutting off everybody.

So it has gone on. The electricity has now been on and off so many times I cannot remember. It seems that each time, the length of time off gets longer and the length of time on gets shorter. As I write, we have been dark for three weeks without a break.

As for water, that comes and goes too. We have learnt to live with buckets prepared. If the water is off, it could be only a day or two days. It makes life a mystery. When you come home at night you ask yourself: "Will there be water or not?" Sometimes you find people washing clothes at night, a thing which was unknown before, in case there is no water in the morning.

What worries many of us is why we in Chiawello 3 are being picked on. In the meantime many other townships have also come in for the same treatment, but not as frequently as us. Is it because the comrades have a low profile in our area? Are we seen as "tame" people who could crack easily?

The impasse is now bothering everybody. Each night one sleeps uncomfortably. People are now used to spending extra money on groceries, the money which was meant to go to the rent. We don't feel the better off, it just all is swallowed in the ever-rising costs. But we worry about how this is going to end. If ever we have to pay the arrears, it will kill people. Even just to resume monthly payments will be nearly impossible for many. But we know we cannot go on having house and services for nothing. No-one is relaxed.

5

Stayaway days

THE dawn of a stayaway breaks much earlier than normal days. One judges the situation by gauging the number of houses lit and street activities such as the number of buses and taxis on the road and the number of people going to the station. One looks for unfamiliar sights, but in most cases by seven there is usually such calm that one may be mistaken into thinking it's Sunday.

On the April stayaway days some people had been woken by a lowflying SADF helicopter reassuring protection and urging people to go to work. The dropping of pamphlets followed. At this time, a number of townships had their electricity cut off and evictions had been effected in some areas. Pamphlet dropping and SADF reassurance did not allay people's fears.

Anyway, on the stayaway days some did go to work, while others remained in the townships.

Stayaways are ambiguous days. Everyone is led by gut feelings. There is no longer any caucusing or conferring with a neighbour on which line of action to take. Over the years we have got to know which neighbours toe which line, and come stayaway morning they each go separate ways.

Also important is the fact that nobody points a finger at whoever has decided to go to work. (Once done, however, you can earn a reputation of being difficult and the punishment could be anything.)

There is empathy among people, as though to say the final decision has to be made by the individual. After all what is the point of pledging loyalty and claiming to stand by the cause when the next day your boss gives you your marching orders. There is nothing neighbours can do to help. On the other hand, supposing you get assaulted on the way from work, you cannot turn around and blame your boss. It is a chance one takes.

One of the striking features on a stayaway day is people's dress — especially those who commute by motor car. They usually dress casually to give the impression that they are home for the day and then quietly sneak out through unfamiliar roads and drive to town. This goes for ordinary commuters too, who on such occasion will wear track suits and pretend to be home or out on a jogging spree.

Fatcats who are not known to be health fanatics, preferring to spend their time in shebeens, also go in for this form of disguise. But, who dares question their sudden love of running? Such people disappear from the township before dawn and can be seen sauntering back around noon from the station or bus stop as if they have simply been wandering around.

By two, all those who have agreeable bosses are back home and are about their business as if they have been home all day. Here and there, neighbours stop and chat, conducting a post-mortem of the day's activities.

The mood around five takes a different shape. Now come the people with hard-hearted bosses, and the people who could not sacrifice wages. There is a heavy presence of casspirs and police at the stations and access routes. Although it has this year become rare to see cars being set alight, it is quite common to see people running away from a scene where somebody's being stoned for having gone to work. It is at such times that one wonders where the large numbers of army trucks are patrolling. This was particularly the case recently at Chiawello station when a woman was clubbed to death coming from work, while Chiawello is always thick with casspirs. It is after all the closest township to the police headquarters.

What takes the cake is watching news on television. You sit and listen to their gospel according to what they want to have happened, which has nothing to do with what you know happened. With poker-straight faces, the presenters talk about our surroundings as though they are referring to some strange land. In fact over the years I have always been amused by the one o'clock news where the presenter would say "all was quiet in Soweto as people flocked to work."

As he speaks, an army helicopter hovers over my roof.

27

6

Working on the railway

THE SATS strike took a toll not only on the railway workers but also on commuters. People died and trains were set alight. Most people who use trains were no longer doing so; there was a scramble for buses and taxis. My station, which under normal circumstances is a hub of activity, was no different from a graveyard. The familiar faces of barrier attendants, booking clerks and labourers were missing. So were even the pair of Railway Police constables who parade up and down the platforms, stern and vigilant in their immaculate uniforms. All of them had been replaced by soldiers with long faces carrying rifles.

I wanted to find some railway workers who would tell me their own stories, rather than the press-statement material. Once it was easy to do this sort of thing. People were keen to speak to reporters, even honoured to have someone taking an interest. Now that is no longer the case. People are scared. You say you are a journalist, it's as if you have a plague.

One day there was a Union meeting at Lekton House. I went down to Wanderers Street. Lo, it seemed like the whole of Africa was there. Hundreds of people milled in the street. Pedestrians, especially whites, were hurrying by nervously, thinking something dramatic was about to happen. People were wondering aloud when the police were going to come. But in fact the strikers were quite harmless, just talking and waiting for someone to tell them what was happening to the strike.

The lift was not working, there was a queue from the street

moving up the stairs to the second floor, where the union, SARWHU, was temporarily housed since Cosatu House had been bombed. (Lekton House is the headquarters of the "enemy", the black consciousness movement and its union allies. I was interested that in a crisis the needs of the workers apparently rise above the ideological disputes.)

I dared not approach the men in the street and ask questions. I had to get into the building and fish out one of the Union leaders to introduce me to the workers.

I started on the long climb up the stairs. Although this building is right in the centre of Johannesburg it happens not to be a modern building. The lifts are most times out of order and the steps are steep and narrow — and now they were sardine-packed with anxious frustrated railwaymen. I wiggled my way up. Keeping my face on my bag and the ground, I elbowed and edged my way between the squashed-up throng. It was hot and the windows were closed. Sweat was coming down my spine and legs. At one point, all movement stopped. We all stood stockstill for what seemed like eternity, not knowing what had created the bottleneck. The smell of perspiration was frightening and tempers were running high as people screamed at the ones ahead to move on.

Although I was part of this hysterical situation I was somehow removed. I was on another plane. Everyone was shouting for things to get moving, while I was paralysed by other worries. Imagine the police coming and saying "three minutes to disperse". They could just as well say "take wings and fly," and in this place the teargas would be murder.

That led to thoughts of a bomb going off. It had happened at Cosatu House only days before, and it could easily do so here. I suppose if I became "journalist who died in the course of duty," I would get a big funeral and be some sort of martyr. But right then that thought was not exciting. All I wanted was to get out, but when it eventually became possible to move there was only one way to go, up.

Then I was on the second floor, which was also teeming with people. A queue marshall screened people on their needs. I extricated myself and kidnapped one of the leaders, who reluctantly agreed to introduce me to strikers. Despite his presence, workers were not welcoming. Many gave us hostile looks, and we moved on without bringing up the subject.

Finally we found two guys who begrudgingly agreed to talk, on condition I was not to know their names. The unionist gave us an office and left us alone. It was like trying to squeeze water out of a stone. The guys were treading very carefully. I got the feeling that it was not only myself they mistrusted, but they were also wary that each other might note down anything which might not be viewed in a good light by their Union. A few years ago, if you were speaking on sensitive issues, people would be similarly worried about things which might not endear them with the System.

These two guys were barrier attendants. During the strike they were living on the money they had saved, not starving like the labourers were. They spoke of terrible working conditions at SATS and said people were not workers but slaves. They were bitter and angry and the only weapon they thought right to solve their problem was the strike. They said the strike had brought up their level, becoming a people's struggle for equality and dignity. They did not seem bothered that the strike was going on and on. They were sure that in the end they were going to win, and were proud of the union for leading them. But then, they spoke from a position of privilege, in that they had money stashed away in the bank.

I asked for details of the bad working conditions. They said one problem was the long working hours, the other and bigger was that the whites called them "kaffirs". I asked about wage problems, but they quickly glossed over and returned to the matter of the whites' attitudes and being called kaffirs. They also complained about a "court" which deals with discipline at SATS. "At this court there are no blacks to listen to our point of view. Only white people with an interpreter. They judge a worker and fine him according to their whims. We do not even know where that money goes to."

From these two I got the impression that 95% of what was troubling them was the way they were treated by white supervisors.

To me this was an irony, because barrier attendants are known by everyone to have a terrible attitude towards commuters. I asked them: If they were so upset because the whites were rude to them, why don't they stop being rude and churlish to the passengers? They didn't know what I was talking about.

Then I wanted their views on the people who had been found dead. Immediately, they started shouting at me. "What do you want to know from us? Have you been sent by the boers? We do not know who killed those people and it has nothing to do with us."

I calmed them down by convincing them I was only interested in knowning the truth, and not in advancing the "line" of any side. After some time they were able to rationalise over the killings. They told me the people who had been killed were scabs. If scabs were left to do as they please then there would be no end to the workers' problems. They gave me a long speech on the wrong of some people who return to work when others are on strike.

30

In the township later that day I met one of the barrier attendants who normally works at my station. He has a girlfriend in my neighbourhood and had been frequenting the place during the strike. He was wearing his black serge uniform trousers, but no jacket or SATS cap, which in the pre-strike period he had worn all the time. In fact they live in them. I knew that he was one of those who had re-applied for his job and I was keen to hear his story. He was looking forward to the court case, coming up in a few days, which he hoped would bring about the end to the strike.

He said that for as long as other workers were not back at their jobs there was no way people like him could hope to work — "We are scared. But this boycott could go on forever. What will my children eat, how will I pay the school fees? For me it is even worse because I stay in a Railway house. If I lose the house, where will I stay?"

I almost told him he was not the only one but I decided against doing so. We all think our problems are worse than everyone else's, after all. I tried to understand his case. He was from Giyani. Losing a job meant forfeiting accommodation. This would mean going to the homelands, it would mean his wife who works in a factory in Johannesburg would have to quit her job too or go rent a room or move to the hostel. It also meant the children would have to leave the local school mid-year and go to the homelands. They would have to acclimatise to a new lifestyle. He had my sympathies.

During the strike my street acquired new neighbours — soldiers.

I came back from work one day to find that a hippo had parked three houses away, dropping off soldiers. What could they want? The registered tenant there is a docile Muslim guy whose only preoccupations in life are middle-aged women and fixing cars. Don't tell me they also think he is a commy.

The next day one of my neighbours disturbed my morning peace: "MaMathiane, do you know that short man is in trouble? Apparently he rented a room to a railway worker, one of those people who scabbed and they caught him. Just before they could necklace him he escaped. I believe the hippos are here to watch the house in case they come for him. In the meantime do you know what he had done? He packed all his belongings and ran off to Venda. Now the poor short fellow has to live with the soldiers."

For almost a month we had the soldiers. We never knew what happened to them at night but during the day, the white ones would sit on chairs outside the house while the black ones wandered around the street, going to the station and coming back with bread and all sorts of victuals. We got used to seeing casspirs loading and off-loading soldiers and the practice was soon dubbed "The Changing of the Guards".

The soldiers did not particularly intimidate anybody. One occasion when playing with one of the boys, they threw a stone at him which broke a neighbour's window. She stormed out like a cyclone. It was as if she had been waiting for them to make one false move. She is a tiny thin-boned woman who you could blow over like blowing out a candle, and she tongue-lashed these fat strong boerboys with their fearsome guns on their shoulders, while they stood with tails between their legs. The whole street was in stitches.

Another person who was affected was one of the shebeen owners, who when the soldiers discovered he was selling liquor, started frequenting his house. One day they demanded free liquor and when he refused they manhandled him. He simply stopped selling.

We woke up one day and the soldiers were gone, but the strike still continued. Trains were being set alight, stories and rumours of deaths and assaults increased and a solution seemed as remote as ever.

There were no railway workers at black stations. People boarded trains without tickets and paid in town. Soldiers were manning most stations. They stood in lines pointing their guns at trains, making us all feel nervous, and irritated. One student remarked that "they have moved from the school yards to the stations."

At New Canada, on several occasions soldiers threw teargas cannisters into moving trains, usually just as the trains pulled off. There would be pandemonium as people choked from teargas. Such actions antagonised commuters from wanting to use the trains and brought them closer to the workers. They stood even more with the workers as they argued SATS was not only exploiting its workers but it was also giving the commuter a raw deal. Increased fares, unhealthy toilets and waiting rooms and a strong possibility of being teargassed made SATS very unpopular.

Whisky all the way

Monday 27 July, Midway station is once more pulsating with life. The men in brown overalls are busy doing maintenance work on the station, the barrier attendant's clipper keeps clicking. The gardener is preparing for spring as he prunes the shrubs and waters the flowers on the station.

But today is not an ordinary day. It is pay day and the first pay day after the four-month strike. One by one workers come back from the paymaster wearing smiles on their faces. The sufferings of the protracted work boycott is paying off. A truck driver who before the strike earned R700 laughs loud as he reads R1 150 reflected on his pay slip. There is jubilation, except among the scabs, who keep to themselves, not even showing their slips to anyone.

Having pocketed their pay slips, most of the labourers vanished from the face of the station. They, unlike the higher ranks, can leave for a special occasion without disrupting affairs. Next port of call is Lenasia, which happens to be the town nearest for cashing cheques. Here they quickly get cash and move into the Lenasia hotel where they order expensive drinks — whisky and beer. A rowdy, however healthy, scene prevails as with glasses bottoms up, the men look back at the past four months, a time when their jobs and lives hung in the balance.

One of the people to have been affected by the strike is the owner of the large tuck shop at the station. His shop sells from chewing gum to paraffin. From a box of matches to mielie meal. The back has been converted to a dining-cum-waiting room. He nearly closed down in the strike. With no workers and no-one boarding trains, business came to a standstill, but his rent still had to be paid. Now he is slowly recovering. But today, everyone is at Lenz. "They will start drinking this [pointing to African beer] mid-month when their coffers run dry. For now it's whisky all the way."

The boers have changed

I spoke to a man of 47. He joined SATS in 1981 as a labourer. Two years ago he was transferred from working on the tracks to becoming a gardener for one of the white supervisors. "I start work in the morning at 7h00 and knock off at 5 p.m. I look after my boss' garden, wash his van and feed the cats and dog.

"I didn't get an increase like the rest of the men. I was one of many who didn't get it although we were told we would get it this month. There was some problem with papers, and I'm sure it will be coming from next month. Many people laughed all the way to the bank yesterday.

"On the subject of the strike I am not very happy with the manner in which it was conducted. For instance we were never formally told about it and the reasons for it. I heard about it through rumour. It was rumoured at the compound that some Venda fellow had been fired and that the next day it was to be tools down. No trade union representative addressed us about it. Just then people died and it became obvious that going to work was not the best thing to do. I joined the strikers and attended meetings to hear for myself what the strike was all about.

"Personally I have no work problems with my boss. I hardly ever see him. He leaves his house around 9 and is back around 3. There is a separate servant working in the house. I realised that many of my colleagues did have problems after attending strike meetings and hearing what they were going through.

"I come from Pietersburg where I have a wife and two children. They are entirely dependent on me. My main concern was what would happen to my family if I lost my job. I am not young or educated, I cannot hop from one job to another. Who would want to employ a man as old as I am? So losing my job would mean my children would have to leave school and look for work. I used to sit at night and think about these things. I do not want my children to lead the life which I as an uneducated man have led. I do not for a moment enjoy living in a compound. I hate being away from my family but to avoid exposing my wife to hunger and my children to a life without education, I have opted for life in the compounds.

"On the bright side I got a lot of strength from my colleagues during the strike. As I sat at night agonising alone on my bed, the next person would be doing the same thing. We were all not sure if it was the right thing to do and there were times when we would be on the verge of breaking, but come morning at the meetings, the leaders would revive our flagging spirits, telling us that victory was in sight.

"Some days we would see some of our colleagues who had not joined us receiving their pay slips, and we felt sore. We were starving and they were eating. Our children were going without food when their children ate. We felt bitter and hated them. Today, they are suffering and management does not know what to with them. We refuse to associate with spineless dogs. Because of their scabbing the strike was prolonged. What hurts even more is that they knew that our fight was theirs as well.

"What I do not understand about scabs is that most of them were educated people who ought to know better than I, being an illiterate. I am told they have big houses in the township and were afraid to lose them. We were also worried about losing our source of livelihood yet we went ahead and downed tools.

"We know exactly who was working and who was not. Our colleagues used to patrol the railway dressed as ordinary commuters to see who was working. We do feel bitter about them. It is not that there is violence, but we ostracise those people. If there is a squad travelling in a truck, we will not let the scabs ride with us.

"Many things have come right since the strike. Even the attitude of the boers has changed. They no longer call us kaffirs and I saw

34

the pay-packets of many people yesterday. They received the promised increase. So what started at Gezina and appeared to be none of my business has worked out in everybody's favour."

7

Waiting for the knock on the door

ONE Friday afternoon in May I walked into my office and was told that the Soweto phones had been cut off again. A friend, Thoko, was with me. She panicked immediately. "They will be detaining people tonight. I spent four months in detention last year, I am not prepared to go in again. I am not going home."

My head spun. My mind went quickly back to the last time the phones were cut off. That was 16 June 1986.

The emergency had just been imposed, many people had been detained. Everybody was anxious. As we left from work the previous day, the 15th, someone said: "Chaps, I don't think there will still be Soweto after tomorrow. The SADF is just going to drop a bomb and wipe us all out." We laughed as we South Africans have grown accustomed to laughing off everything lest we go mad, but we never knew when (or if) we were going to see each other again. I promised to phone my colleagues to let them know I was alright.

Came 16 June, the sun rose as usual and I went out to study the situation as we usually do on Stay-Aways. My neighbour was out sweeping her yard, there were men congregated in small groups looking towards the main road, from whence the army cars usually appear.

I wanted to know how my sister in Rockville was doing. I went to the telephone and picked it up. It was dead. I hit on the bar to get the dialling tone like a mad person, but the phone remained dead. Incredible. I was up-to-date with my payments: what could be wrong? This had never happened before. Through the window I called my neighbour and asked her if her phone was working. She told me it was. I insisted that she check. She went into the house and came back with a look that told the story. It was not working. So that was it.

We spent the day in limbo, not knowing what was happening even in the next township let alone the country, the radio giving us only the usual.

I have miserly relatives who phone me only on my birthday and on 16 June and whenever there are new spates of stories about Soweto revolts. My mother is one of these, I imagined the frustration she suffered down in Zululand, trying to reach her various children in Soweto. We survived the day seeing army cars going in and out of the locations. Occasionally one could see young people running away from the army vehicles but generally it was quiet.

The next day, upon getting to work and once again being in communication, I was amazed at the anger the cutting off of the phones had evoked. People were saying things like "who do the boers think they are to deny us the use of the telephones that we rent?" Somebody suggested that we take all the phones and dump them at the post office. Others wanted to know if we would be credited for the 24 hours that the phones were not working.

So, while Thoko was going on about booking into a hotel, I was reliving 16 June 1986.

In typical ignorant white fashion my colleague wanted to know why they would pick Thoko up. Thoko explained that she had been involved in street committees last year. "Once they detain you, there is no guarantee they might not do so again." My colleague looked at me. I feared she might say something stupid such as "but Nomavenda was also in a street committee, why isn't she being picked up?" This would just frighten Thoko even more.

Staying in a hotel was not the answer, alone in a strange place in town, unable even to phone through to Soweto. In Soweto, we can at least share our problems. I said Thoko should spend the night with me, where we can drive around and get to know what the boers are getting at. She agreed and we set off for home.

Many years ago when Thoko started teaching, I was already a journalist. I liked her but was terribly irritated by the simplicity of her thinking. She was neither political nor unaware. She seemed content with the knowledge that she was black and underprivileged. She used to take me to task for being so outspoken. She would say, "we know all what you are talking about. Some of us are not talkers, we are action people, tell us what to do and then judge us from there." Did I have the answers? No.

Came 1985, there was chaos in the country. People were being detained and others being killed. Comrades and com-tsotsis emerged. Cars were forcefully taken away from owners, people were necklaced, houses were set alight, students were fighting among themselves, house rentals were boycotted. The councillors were evicting residents and, in turn residents resisted evictions.

It was with that kind of climate that street committees were born. In some areas, street committees happened as a natural process and at others they were initiated by comrades. In Thoko's area, it was the people who decided their township was going to the dogs and they needed to get together and fight the elements that were causing them sleepless nights. So they got together and formed themselves into street committees.

Of course not everything was hunky-dory after that. But some semblance of order emerged. And soon the security police became interested.

Just before 16 June, they began round-ups. Thoko came to see me. She was on her way to the library. She said that one of the bigwigs in the UDF had called. He said it seemed that they were taking everyone who was in street committees. He advised that she take to her heels as he was going to do so. I asked her what was she waiting for. Her answer was that she first wanted to loan a few books that she had long been meaning to read and then go hibernating in some homeland. I told her she was playing games with the system. If word was out that they were coming for her then she had better run now or wait to face the detention. She promised to move out the next day. I said this was a mistake. She said no, she was just a little fish and would be well in time.

That night, she later told me, she woke up to torches all over and the knock on the door. She ran to her parents' bedroom and told them to tell the cops she was not around. Then she climbed into the ceiling.

Her parents went to the door. The cops asked for Thoko. Before her mother could answer, her father shouted "Come out, Thoko, they want you. I do not harbour criminals in my house. If you have done nothing then come out and face these men." And as he was saying so, he was moving towards the trap door in the ceiling and the police were behind him.

You would think she would be angry with her father, but she told me that she actually laughed. "It was so typical of Papa," she said later, "he was such an honest person."

She collected her washing cloth and toothbrush and kissed her parents goodbye. Her father tried to inquire why they were taking her away and was told "routine questioning".

Thoko spent four months in prison when one Saturday morning, after breakfast, she was told to get out of her cell. The chief warder told her she was being released. She was driven home in a van.

She was not given reasons for her release. On the way home, the van stopped in an open veld and the policeman told her she was being taken home but there was something they wanted her to do for them. She could live on easy street for the rest of her life if she would tell them of some of the things that go on in her township.

Thoko was furious. "I could not understand the logic of this man. I had spent four months in solitary confinement for doing nothing but being involved in street committees, which gave us the means to put our township in order. Now this man was asking me to inform for them. How stupid can some people be," she said. She then told him to rather take her back to her cell. But they proceeded on to her home.

As she arrived at her street, she noticed people around her home. At first she thought maybe they had heard (which was unlikely) of her release. But as the van stopped she noticed the window panes were smeared with grey to indicate there was a funeral.

Her immediate reaction was not to get out of the van. She didn't want to know who might be dead. She could not imagine her world without any of her sisters or brothers, let alone mother or father.

Jelly knees carried her into the house where she found friends and relatives from near and far. What was strange was the manner in which they regarded her. They greeted her as though she had come back from town or somewhere near. Not that she expected a hero's welcome but the cold manner in which she was being treated was rather strange behaviour. Her friends seemed to avoid meeting her eyes, nor were they warm towards her as someone they had not seen for a long time. "Something funny around here," she thought.

The kitchen was full of women. Some were peeling vegetables and others cooking or taking food outside to be cooked by the men and women tending to the huge furnace especially designed for a large gathering. She pushed her way towards her parents' bedroom. There was her mom seated on the mattress amidst a group of women. A coffin lay beside them. Nobody had to tell her. It was her father after all. The rest she does not remember as women started wailing while some were busy reviving her.

Among her many friends present was Dimakatso Pooe. In fact their relationship had long transcended that of mere friendship. They were sisters. Thoko is, in fact, Dimakatso's protegé.

Having both grown up in Pimville and achieved certain goals the community looks up to the two girls and is proud of them.

And yet on that fateful Saturday, the usually garrulous Dimakatso seemed withdrawn and aloof. She went about the duties, serving tea and making mourners comfortable without mixing with the other women. I noticed that and thought it was because she was so close to the family, maybe the death of the old man was getting her down.

It was only when we were at the graveside that I began to get wind of what was actually going on. Apparently, some people had spread around the story that Dimakatso together with Thoko's mom, had sold Thoko out. The reason, these people said was to get at Thoko's father who adored her over all her other children.

Well, that did not make sense to me. I could not for the love of anything think of any woman who could sell out her daughter. Secondly, I could not see Dimakatso ever selling out on anything or anyone. She was just not that type. I also could not understand the logic. How could Thoko's detention be used as a weapon to get even with her father?

I shuddered. At the time Dimakatso was riding on the crest of fame being a member of the Soweto Parents Crisis Committee. It was quite obvious to me that there were certain personalities who felt jealous of her success and recognition. How many people have fallen victim to such slander and been necklaced? All we needed was some mad person to incite the people. I went cold.

At the graveyard, Thoko was in the dark. It was as we came back to the house that someone told her that Dimakatso was supposed to have betrayed her. I suppose they hoped that she would shun Dimakatso. In fact she went straight over and hugged her and they cried.

What a moving sight. Especially because everybody knew how false the rumour was. It had been intended to destroy Dimakatso. But in times of necklaces who dared question people telling stories. It was more of the story of "For whom the bell tolls" and hope it never does for you.

Thoko's father had been stabbed by unknown people not far from his house as he was coming back from a funeral vigil in the next street. Early risers to work had stumbled on to the corpse on their way to the station and had alerted the police.

In a way, her father's death was to me more painful than many I had heard of lately. It had become so common to bury people who had died from bullets that his death did not make sense.

To me it seemed incongruous that while we were building all sorts of protection structures against the governing system this old man had to die at the hands of his children for no reason.

I actually felt the physical pain somewhere next to my ribcage as I listened to the sermon promising of a better life than the one he had been leading. I was angry. We could not go on like this. How cheap could life be? What were we to tell our grandchildren? Psychologists were forever analysing the situation and blaming it on the system. We had heard so much of that and as a result we believed it was not our responsibility. How long would we continue to hide behind the veil of the system and exterminate each other?

I return to that day in May when I was taking Thoko to my house.

As we drove into my yard my neighbour came up. She said: "Daisy [one of her daughters] was collected this morning for her involvement in street committees. They asked for you too, so you had better be ready."

At this, Thoko saw the funny side. Everyone was involved, so what was the point of hiding? In hysterics with laughter, she yelled at me: "You bitch, fancy saying I should come with you when you knew very well that we were both in the same boat."

What else could we do but laugh and hope they do not come for us? They did not.

When writing this piece I did not feel comfortable using people's real names. Many people suffered last year and many wounds have not yet healed. A lot of suspicion prevails and journalists face the arduous task of having to tread very carefully. Without real leadership our society has developed some unpleasant characteristics – one of which is finger pointing and witch-hunting.

8

Picnic in the park

ON the morning of Kruger Day — Saturday, 10 October — there were groups with picnic equipment waiting for taxis at arranged places around the township.

Now, Kruger Day was showing that a new era was on the way. It was the first public holiday of summer. The comrades had become a thing of the past. I recognised some of the people waiting for the taxis as ex-comrades. It was amusing to watch the same youngsters who only a few months back had put the fear of God into us so changed. For was it not last year this time when they were knocking at our doors with all sorts of demands? Yes people change and times change.

So, it was the first picnic of the year, but much more than that, once more our children were being children — going out and having fun.

In the evening there was a great amount of excitement as the crowds returned. Many were chatting away, while many others were too drunk to know where they were. Such is the fun of today's youngsters.

On Sunday, stories of untoward behaviour started making the rounds. Rumour had it that the kids who had gone to picnic in white areas had been disgustingly drunk, making absolute fools of themselves. Some had been admitted at Baragwanath hospital where surgery had to be performed immediately.

Most people shrugged their shoulders. People do not like to hear these stories, but they are not surprised. We know it is a fact that the kids will stab each other at picnics.

When picnicking means the packing of liquor and weapons what can one really expect? It has become sort of a norm that when children go to picnics, some get hurt while others die, some may escape this time but they may not next time. There is also the element of revenge which plays an important part.

It is not as if parents do not know that picnics are a great excuse for getting far away, well stocked with liquor and food and equally well protected with arms, "just in case". Moreover with the white parks now accepting blacks there is always the chance that one township gang will unintentionally bump into a rival group which has chosen the same spot — remember "great minds".

Besides there are some places where blacks are more at home than others, and there are some customs which people have grown used to. The Wilds is for wedding parties to take photographs and for old people. Parents who want to combine a peaceful time with some education for children make their way to Pretoria Zoo. Wemmer Pan, the Zoo Lake and the Lion Park are the places you go if you want noise and dancing and are not too worried about the risk of violence breaking out.

One would wonder why the kids prefer to go to white spots when there are ever so many parks in Soweto. The answer is simple, they are not parks but death traps.

How many times have early risers stumbled onto corpses lying at Thokoza park in Rockville or at the Mofolo park.

Mofolo park is famous for people washing their cars and for secret lovers committing adultery in locked cars under the trees. For respectable people it is unthinkable that you could go to Mofolo or Thokoza and have a picnic with your children. It does not even cross your mind. People do not see these places as parks in the same way that they see the Zoo Lake and the other real parks in town. Mofolo and Thokoza are just open spaces with trees, and thoroughfares between townships.

As for the Oppenheimer park — that has never been seen as part of Soweto. It has always been for the white tourists to end their trip of Soweto by looking down at us from the tower. After 1976, the West Rand Board blundered even more by giving part of it over to Credo Mutwa to create a "khaya" museum of some sorts. This is for whites on the bus tours to visit. Local residents do not even know that the park exists. They see the tower, and they believe that it is a soldier's memorial of some sort.

After living in Soweto for my whole life, I only discovered this park in 1980 when I was taken there by whites who were showing a foreign visitor around.

The rest of the parks are mainly used as thoroughfares. Few have any trees or grass, never mind water. A year or two years ago the comrades had their famous campaign to clean up the townships. I must say that they did put in a good effort. We ended up with lots of clean spaces where there had been nothing but dumps before.

This had its own problems. People were forced to provide money for paint. We suspected that the money did not all go towards paint, but those were the days when we dared not question. Anyhow, we did see that there was much use of paint. A big stone or boulder would be painted yellow or black and there would be a sign saying "Welcome to Zoro Park — do not walk here" or something like that.

Whatever the problems, there is no doubt that the empty spaces were cleaned up. Now they have gone back to the old state. But even when clean, they were never really parks.

So there is no local park for picnics. Even if there was, Soweto is so depressing, with the same sights of rows and rows of identical houses and identical combi taxis and identical Putco buses day after day, that people would still want to get a breath of fresh air elsewhere. They would still go to the white parks even if the government built a complete new Zoo Lake in Soweto.

It should be remembered that not all black children subscribe to the picnic world. There are those who are into soccer, youth clubs, doing plays, or going to musical festivals.

Of these, the youth-club set are by far the most peaceful. They are respectful and education-oriented, and anybody who touches any liquor, even a glass of beer, is frowned upon.

The type that goes to musicals is basically non-violent and rarely carries any form of weapon. Also the festivals will show a good range in generation, from teenager to middle-aged. There can be fist fights, especially if liquor flows, but seldom more than that.

The soccer crowd are mainly harmless. It is in the picnic set that the violence is great. Boys can be strolling about as friends at noon, and by evening one or two can be at the mortuary.

On Monday morning I was shocked to see the white papers — *The Citizen* and the Afrikaans paper *Beeld*. They had huge reports about blacks going on the rampage. It was like the report of a war starting.

There were moving pictures of people bleeding and their sad stories. But I also knew for a fact that there were black people who had died and no mention was made of them in the papers. Was that not news worth mentioning? Or was this the objectivity the liberal press keeps talking about?

What actually happened? I thought *The Sowetan* would throw some light into the matter. I searched in vain: *The Sowetan* did not even mention it.

I went to Zondi township where I had been told there were victims. I collected a friend who stays in the area and we asked what had happened. Most people did not want to talk about the drunken boys who went to town and started killing each other. "They had no business to go to the picnic drunk as they were," said one parent. Another person blamed it on some Portuguese guys who were selling liquor at the park. "What did they expect. Of course they went there to make the people get drunk. What did they want to happen?"

Most people knew nothing about whites being killed. Only a few had seen it in the white newspapers. It was not a talking point. The talking point was that black kids had gone all the way to town to kill each other. That was something new. And people were sorrowful that here was trouble again. We know that things will never be truly normal. We will always fear the next uprising, and wonder what form it will take. But we had a short glimpse of a semblance of normality that Saturday. We had been secretly hoping for the best, and now it had gone wrong.

Some people put the blame squarely on the police. "The children were drunk and waiting for their transport when the police came and opened tear gas. You know how our children don't want to see the sight of the police. They went mad. The police provoked the kids as usual. If they had left the kids alone, their transport would have eventually come for them and taken them home instead of wandering the streets of Johannesburg and slashing people's throats," said one.

One thing I know is the effect police have over black youth. If the police have guns, then they get even wilder. Their dealings with the cops have made them to know the number of bullets police guns carry. And as the police shoot they are ducking and counting. Once they know the last shot has been fired they advance. So it is quite often not wise to bring in the cops.

I could also understand the adverse role played by the white guys who came selling beers. The kids had taken enough drink to the park already. What the white guys had actually done was to exacerbate the situation by replenishing them. Under normal circumstances, one would argue they were providing a service, but we don't need that type of a service. But how do they get it right to stand there in front of a park and peddle liquor, a mobile bottle store? Can anybody do that in a black area? No ways.

If the bootleggers had not been there, the kids would have run out of stock, slept, woken up babbelaased, and gone home. But now you had them demanding more, with no money to pay. The white bootleggers panicked and asked for the only help they can rely on to deal with blacks — the law. Unfortunately the police have over the years proved not to be capable of handling skirmishes of this nature. In many cases they have made mountains out of moles.

But if you have seen children at work you will understand why the Portuguese panicked.

I have seen a Greek shop swept clean by school kids on an excursion. As they enter the shop, the girls flock to the counter and confuse the one at the counter. This is probably in some country town — you cannot try this trick with Harry Sam! The shopkeeper is confused, seeing so many customers. While he is attending to the girls screaming for this and that he is not aware that the boys in the background are removing items such as bags of oranges and crates of soft drinks. One told me of how he stole a bucket of ice-cream and tried to sell it to his mates in the bus. Of course they refused to buy as they knew he had stolen it and wanted it for free. In the end he had to relent and give it away before it melted.

I went to the home of one of the victims. I looked at this seventeen-year-old who looks thirteen and I couldn't imagine him drunk. He looked so small, like a little child to be sent to the shops, not like someone who could lift a beer-can.

He could not recall what happened. He was too drunk to know. Apparently he just lay there as he was being stabbed. His mother would not allow us to speak to him, saying they had been summoned to go to the police station.

"Except that I do not understand why our children who have been stabbed have to be questioned, when the police's job is to find the people responsible for all this fracas."

This woman's neighbour's son, aged 15, had been stabbed to death on the picnic. Another boy from the same street came home with a knife buried in his forehead, between the eyes. He was then taken to Baragwanath, where doctors performed a miraculous operation. The woman said the police would not release the corpse to the parents, because they wanted to examine any possible "political" connections. She was very angry about this, asking since when do they keep corpses from the family.

We were listening to the woman when one of the neighbours' sons walked in. He had also been to the picnic. He said: "I heard my brother scream that this one was being injured and saw him rush to his assistance. The next thing a knife was plunged into my brother. The attacker ran off. I ran looking for transport to take the two to the hospital. Then there was chaos as the police came and chased people with tear gas. People were rushing to put their belongings together

46

— provision baskets and music sets had to be packed in a hurry. There was tear smoke and bleeding people all around."

My friend and I moved from the victim's house to the local shops. We found a group engaged in conversation. I asked if they could explain what happened on Saturday. One of them wanted to know who I was. I mumbled that I was a reporter. He threw a copy of the *Citizen* at me and asked "Did you write this?" I shook my head. I told him who I worked for.

One of the boys took two steps and stood right in front of me, aggressively. "You are a comrade," he said. "Did you not raid so-and-so's house . . .?"

My palate went dry. He was referring to an occasion where I had been very embarrassed to find myself caught up, in the course of duty, in a raid by comrades. I had hoped against hope that nobody would remember me. But now it seemed the chickens were coming home to roost. I explained: "I am not a comrade. And I was at that house as a reporter. Just as I am here to listen to your side of the story." He seemed satisfied.

"What do you want to know? That we went out on a picnic and we were butchered like cows? I cannot tell you what happened but in the afternoon, we were all so high and there was our friend S'khumbuzo on the ground dead and others bleeding. It was bad," said a boy.

"We were enjoying ourselves, drinking beers and listening to music when two Portuguese guys arrived in a van selling liquor. By the evening many guys were drunk but still wanted some more to drink. At that stage most had run out of money. Some started playing rough with the Portuguese wanting to take beers for free.

"A nasty scene was imminent so the police were called. These arrived and teargassed everyone. There was no transport to bring us back home as we had instructed our taxis to pick us up around six. So there we were, teargassed to go away, where to, anywhere. Some resisted being chased away and hit back at whatever was in their way. So, here we are, without a brother and we don't even know who killed him."

I found out that the whole group were school going kids. They were either doing standard nine or ten, and between fifteen and twenty years old. They seem to be into beer drinking and once drunk they were uncontrollable. One of them, I was told, had tried to rape a girl not far from his home on returning from the picnic. In fact the girl had been saved by his parents who came out on hearing screams.

It also transpired that at the school they attend, one of the boys had decapitated a classmate and the boys had spent the entire day combing the townships looking for the culprit.

An elderly witness claims the children were too drunk to know what was going on. He saw one being stabbed, and maintains it was to the good that they were so drunk. He lay there drunk while he was being stabbed. Had he been in his senses he would have pulled his own knife and there could have been another two deaths. As it was, the one ended up with many stab wounds in his buttocks.

The tragedy is the position of the parents. It is not as if parents do not know what happens at these picnics. They can do nothing about their children's behaviour. How does the parent go against the tide?

The kids have to protect themselves against many systems, using different weapons. At home silence may be the best weapon to get nosy parents off one's back. At school the choice is between killing time as best as one can and relying on the new slogan of "Pass One, Pass All", or getting on with the job and being resented as a "beterkoffie" or sell-out. In the street it is either joining the gang (carrying knives, harassing girls and getting drunk) or be seen as "barrie" (bum) and be humiliated for not being "with it".

On Saturday S'khumbuzo should have been buried but the funeral did not take place because his mother died of a heart attack on Friday. His sister could not take it. She took poison and is being treated at Baragwanath Hospital.

9

Quiet collapse

WHEN we first heard the call for "Liberation now, Education later," we were told the students were going to stand united until liberation was achieved. What has happened is the opposite. The well-off children have left the township schools. The poor have stayed in the townships, where they have long forgotten education and now have forgotten liberation too. They just roam the streets and sometimes visit the classroom, where they meet their friends and play and chat. There is no secondary education any more, in Soweto and other main townships.

Every parent who could by any means afford it, has removed their children. They have gone to private schools, homeland boarding schools, or to live with relatives. There was a great deal of arm twisting, begging and bribing. Among those to leave were students who incited others not to attend. That is one reason why there were no boycotts in '87. Activists saw their way into private schools, where the spirit of militancy is subdued. One factor being, at such schools they are overshadowed and outnumbered by their white colleagues. Added to that, the learning atmosphere is certainly different.

Aside from the "real" private schools, new schools mushroomed in the city. Students pay anything from R100 per month, and buy books as well as pay for transport into town. Now the township looks different. In the old days streets filled in the early mornings with children dressed in black-and-white uniforms. Today, there are mini-buses ferrying children in the multi-coloured uniforms of the white private schools. Another lot will be the kids going by train and bus to the new schools in the city centre, wearing clean casual gear.

Later in the day come the remaining children, from the township schools. They drift towards school at any time they like, wearing any outfit. Often they look more like thugs than schoolchildren.

During 1987 the school scene was ignored. At the beginning, everybody held their breath to see whether the kids would return to school. Some kids did not register immediately, but gradually it became obvious that they were back at school, and the politicians and newspapers began to lose interest. June 16 came and went without drama, and then people were finally convinced that the school problem was over.

Those who wanted to draw attention to the problems in the class-rooms, kept to themselves for fear of making waves when life was getting normal. Parents preferred to sweep the problems under the carpet. They were relieved that "sayinyova" had come to an end. The children were no longer rampaging and throwing stones. People did not want to disturb things by probing as to what was actually going on. They did not want to ask: why was there no homework any more? Why go to school so late, and back so early? They thought the less one knows, the better. If they did not look, the problem would disappear.

But everybody knew, deep down, that things were wrong.

Mr H H Dlamlenze, general secretary of the African Teachers Asso-ciation of SA (ATASA) was regarded as a moderate and conservative until 1985, when he was detained for six months — because, he suspects, Atasa was planning a commemoration of the 10th anniver-sary of Soweto '76.

Although his tone has much changed, he is still basically a moderate. He continues living his life without lamenting the wasted time and humiliation. He does not speak with the usual ex-detainee rhetoric, and is not even proud of detention.

On the state of today's education he says: "I took a visiting American to a school and asked the principal if we could chat with students. The principal said it was alright by him but he first had to check with the SRC.

"My heart was sore. What has happened to authority? Who is leading who?"

Mr Dlamlenze maintains the teachers are powerless pawns in the game. The students want change and want it now. The parents want the children out of the house and in someone else's care. The govern-ment wants to see them in the classroom to save face. Nobody is winning.

50

A lady teacher concurred: "Granted, we have no control over the students, but it is worse when you find some teachers currying favour with the children. The children get to expect that they can push teachers around. I have been approached on several occasions and threatened that I dare not let them fail my subject."

She cited a 13-year-old boy who had been absent from school for many weeks. Then he was brought back by his mother because he had raped a six-year-old. "His mother appealed to me to take him back to keep him out of harm's way. I had to take him because if I refused there could be a boycott — 'an injury to one is an injury to all.'

"We are meant to be parents as well as teachers. Parents are too scared to preach about morals. They want us to do that, but we have no time set aside for it. The churches also shun that subject. They talk about the soul and preach against witchcraft and adultery, and hope the schools will explain to the growing child what is expected of him — without a syllabus for it!

"The new incoming teacher is a product of 1976. He has been fighting the system as a student and did not get very far. He has an unfinished agenda which he passes on to the children. At times we cannot take important decisions that will affect the students, for fear that our colleagues might tell on us."

One teacher calls it "battle-fatigue". The children are back at school physically and are recuperating from the four years of not learning.

"Learning habits are broken down and it will be some years before we have a generation of children who are at school for the purpose of learning.

"Human beings are not taps that can be switched on and off and the sooner the government learns that no amount of bullets will create a learning atmosphere the better. We have a generation that has been lost. What are we doing to save the next one?"

I called at a school which was at one stage one of the best in Soweto, boasting of teachers with strings of degrees. It was also one of those high schools in the forefront of the 1976 uprisings.

Today the school is a shadow of what it was. The teachers openly describe themselves as "cheque collectors". They are destroyed.

"Soweto is Sodom and Gomorrah," says the headmaster. "This place must be razed to the ground and rebuilt afresh, and not with the present child. These children are poison."

If it was that bad, I said, why was he still teaching? The answer was simple. At over 50, who would employ him? Because the Department forbids teachers to give interviews I cannot name him.

"Come and look at the children's scripts," he said, "they have written nothing because they have not been in the classroom. They have been coming to school when and if they want to. I have requested meetings with parents — these have not been attended. Parents are not interested in knowing whether their children are learning or not. As long as they seem to be away from home it is alright by them."

I looked at a pile of end-of-year exam scripts. What I saw was long blank spaces. A full sheet of paper could have three or four lines filled in. The rest had nothing but question numbers, with no answers next to them. "We also need to look at the social problems, such as the shortage of houses. People have been looting corrugated iron from my school to build shacks. When I confronted the ones I caught red-handed, they asked me: 'What does a child need most, a school or a home?' They said the school was not being used in any case, so why should they not strip the classrooms?"

He said: "In the past we felt hopeless with Bantu Education. Educationalists claimed that the longer a child stayed at school the more difficult it was to undo the harm done by Bantu Education. So year in and year out we churned out a frustrated product. But at least they knew their limitations and worked from that premise. Today, we have a zombie who comes to school, squanders his pocket money at break and goes home without having touched a book. The teacher can do nothing.

"Where does it put the black nation? We are going to be despised by everyone. Bantu Education was inferior but at least a child received some education. In the past, whites sympathised with us because of the poor education we received. Now the opportunities are better, but the children have no goals, no values and no direction. They do not aspire to anything, they are just drifting along."

Another headmaster, a primary school principal, was one of the angriest people I have ever seen. A strong, athletic man, he has no fear, and he blames the collapse on "lily-livered" teachers.

He said there was order in most primary schools. "We break our backs teaching and when our children leave our gates for high school, then we know it is good-bye to education. Teachers fear these kids. I have seen teachers being abused and humiliated by 15-year-olds and doing nothing about it."

I asked him about teachers who have been fatally assaulted by students. He said: "Fear will never solve our problems. A teacher must behave as one and not pander to the children's whims." A maths teacher from a high school said: "We cannot continue fooling ourselves that we will wake up one day and find ourselves leading normal lives. Even teachers have taken their children away — you can't find a Soweto teacher whose child goes to a Soweto school. The government will continue to pretend all is well and keep on suppressing the lid. Education becomes available only to those who can afford private schools. We in the government schools continue collecting our cheques to pay our bonds, but are not earning what we are paid."

I spoke to Mr G.W. Merbold, regional director of the Department of Education and Training. His sole aim is to give the best education to the black child. He does not see education in this country as political and "if you want to politicise it then you can go and talk to the politicians." In other words, he does not want to discuss the impact of political problems on education. "At least in 1987, 83% of registered children did actually sit for the exams.

"I am not very optimistic about the results because the studying patterns of pupils had broken down and we could not water down the examinations to suit the children. We have no intention of bringing down the standards lest we be accused of offering an education that is inferior."

He said black children were receiving free education, of the same quality as white people. There were no school fees paid by parents, and pupils were being given free stationery and books. All a black child had to do was present him or herself to the school and study. The only payment by parents was the school fund which was determined by the school and was voluntary anyway.

"And yet some parents prefer to pay exorbitant amounts at the schools in town."

I asked why would parents pay exorbitant amounts if they could get good education free. He said "You tell me, I don't understand the people's mentality. They run away from schools in black areas, claiming they are getting away from DET, but at the end of the year they sit for our exams."

I said that if black and white education was equal, what was the point of having different departments? He said that was a question, not for him, but for the politicians. He said parity had been reached in pay, subsidies and pension schemes.

Mr Merbold genuinely felt he was doing the right thing for the people, but whether the people realised that, was another matter. It is not the changing of the name from Bantu Education to DET that people wanted. The people were calling for one education for all South African children, and parity in spending. We have seen the many schools that have been built and the free stationery, but these have not meant better learning.

The Department wants to normalise education without dealing with the basic political problems. To me, that is a waste of time. It is not a matter of whether 83% or any other percent of children are sitting in classrooms, it is a matter of whether they are learning how to hold their own in society.

How he can claim to be doing the best for the black child, while he refuses to see the core of the problem, is beyond me. All we are going to have is a cycle of lulls and then storms. The difference is not between progress and collapse. It is between quiet collapse and violent collapse.

Came January 1988 and matric results were announced. There was more scepticism than jubilation. Although there has been a marginal increase in the pass rate — from 53% to 56% as well as an increase in the number of university entrances — however, black parents are not excited. They smell a rat.

People feel that somehow the results are being cooked. For one thing, the director of education Mr G.W. Merbold predicted an improvement on the result. Indeed the result came out better. This was in spite of the lack of learning and the non-commitment of children towards education.

Parents are asking as to who is the department fooling because the situation in Soweto has been such that everybody knew what was going on and yet the result came out as though there has been an effort towards learning. Of course, the children had gone back to school but whether they were learning anything is another matter.

One teacher spoke of "letting the stream flow" which she claimed was a directive from the department that they should allow kids to proceed to the next class so as not to create bottlenecks at high school.

And from the looks of things the situation is going to remain unredressed because already black leaders who would be in a position to tackle the department do not have their children in Soweto schools. They do not feel comfortable to speak on behalf of the ordinary parent whose child is schooling in the township. They have been criticised for wanting to represent other people's children while theirs were not at such schools. So who is going to confront the department?

Already parents are running to and fro trying to find schools outside Soweto. There has been an even larger group of students leaving black schools for the ones in town. Even those in town have experienced a shift from one school to the other. This is in spite of the good results that are alleged to have come out. Where there should have been an exodus of children going back to the ghetto schools, we see them drifting even further away. And the truth of the matter is, children who want to learn have no confidence in black schools.

A tour of inspection

I VISITED Thulare High School in White City Jabavu. This is one of the double-storey buildings which was built after 1976. In the old days, schools were long single-storey "L" shapes, white at the top and maroon below. The new pattern makes schools look different, like barracks.

Thulare stands impressively next to ecumenical centres of the Lutheran and Methodist churches, which give it, from the outside, an appearance of calm and dignity.

Inside, the school is filthy and run down. Some classrooms are without doors. Broken desks lie all over the place. An attempt is made to sweep the floors, but the whole place is grey from lack of polish. The walls compete for inscriptions of rival political groups. The ceiling is marked by ball prints creating a muddy tapestry of what once was a white ceiling. The toilets are no longer used because they are not cleaned. Before the uprisings, students took turns in cleaning toilets. Today there is no child who is prepared to clean toilets.

I went to Orlando High School. For years this school was the pride of Soweto. It has been fondly referred to as "The Rock". Many great people were educated there and some of the best teachers taught there — Prof. Ezekiel Mphahlele, Mr Godfrey Pitje and Mr Ike Moephuli, to mention but a few.

For many years the great Mr TW Khambule was principal. Although Orlando High is in the heart of crime-country, it always stood above crime. Order was its language.

Today many classrooms and toilets (always a separate building) are without rooves as the corrugated iron has been removed. Most cooking equipment in the house-craft centre has been stolen. In some classes, tiles on the floor have been removed and the ceiling in the staff-room has been taken. Pupils do not use the toilets any more.

Beaten by the comrades

I SPOKE to a girl who tried to write matric in 1985. She was turned back by comrades. Her back bears testimony, showing marks from the shambokking she got when she crossed the boycott line.

Once more in 1986 she enrolled to write but they were again told there would be no writing of examinations. This time she did not bother to get to the centre. Came 1987, she registered with both the Adult Centre and day school.

"A teacher with a first period will find that he has three or five students to teach. Suppose he decides to teach, then he has to teach the same thing the next day to those children who were not there the previous day. The following day he may be faced with a different lot. So what do the teachers do? They stay out of class, especially those with early periods. And I don't blame them," she said.

Although her back has black marks from the beatings, she is not bitter. "At first I was very angry. My mother was away at work and I wanted to commit suicide. I was in terrible pain. I could't find tablets or medicine to drink to kill myself. I cried to sleep. When my mother came back my entire back was swollen. She broke down and together we wept. She was worse than me because she kept on calling my father's name asking why did he have to die and leave her with such problems. We felt so helpless. I could not even call any of my male cousins for help because those were the days when students who had braved the comrades and sat for exams were viewed as sell-outs. In the meantime children in other parts of the country were writing as though nothing was happening."

A very determined student

AT Orlando High I met a girl of about 20, who I found out was writing matric.

She started school in 1974. Since then she has experienced seven years of learning ('74-75, '79-83), five years of disruption ('76-77, '84-86) and two years of limbo ('78 and '87). As a primary school child in '76 and '77 her school was closed several times either because high school students came to chase children away or because there was shooting or teargas in the vicinity and the principal sent them home.

"In 1984 the comrades told us not to come to school. They would tear our books and gym dresses. Soon soldiers came into the school grounds and not long after that the school was shut down.

"My parents applied to boarding schools but they would not take me from Johannesburg as I would be a bad influence. I went to a private school.

"When schools were reopened I went back. Some of us were against what the comrades were doing. When we used to confront them about 'liberation now and education later' they would tell us to go to the classroom at our own risk and that we dared not do.

"Students today do as they please. A class can be busy at work in one classroom only to find the next room behaving as if it was at a picnic. Loud music is played and boys and girls frolic about. If you don't like that scene you are advised to get out of the classroom. Most teachers don't bother to come after lunch because there are no children to teach.

"This causes problems for us girls who want to study. It is for this reason that we have formed study groups and conduct house visits. It is not safe for girls to study on their own at school. Some have been raped in the classrooms.

"Everything is left up to the student. Some of the students who were in the front of nyovment [disruptions] are studying again. But there are those who do not want to learn. I have enrolled with the night school in case the call comes again for us to leave the classrooms."

10

The empire strikes back

SOME say the chickens are coming home to roost. Some say people have had a two-year Christmas — paying no rent for all that time, they are supposed to be rich by now. Some say they are stupid and wonder how long did they hope to live rent-free. The residents say "we have been robbed".

One thing is sure. The great rent boycott is collapsing. People used to expect that there would be a big dramatic clampdown. They said that the government would never succeed, because it would face united resistance from a million people. But the government has chosen "softly softly catchee monkey".

All the time, the people have waited for the leaders and the government to come to some agreement. But now the leaders are silenced or silent. The drama has gone, and it has become a matter of the Soweto Council police, protected by the army, picking on selected spots and leaving people rushing to pay the rent.

This month they raided houses in Chiawello 3, demanding rent receipts. Those who did not have current receipts had their furniture thrown into the army trucks and their homes locked up. People were running backwards and forwards looking for leaders, looking for money, pointing fingers at those who were not raided. Streets were piled with televisions, sofas, fridges, food. Women wailed hopelessly. Children watched their beds being flung into trucks. The constables loaded, under the watch of the soldiers, casually chomping at the fruits or sipping drinks from the fridge. The sound of splintering and cracking rings out. Drawers fall out of cupboards, and clothes and cutlery fall out of drawers.

For many months Chiawello residents have been unhappy with the boycott. They have wanted to pay rent, and get rid of the insecurity. But they couldn't just go and pay, they needed the problem resolved.

Chiawello 3 has been cursed by rent confusion since the township was built in 1982. Residents were told they would pay R145,20 provisional rent for six months. Then the amount would be reviewed.

After six months, nothing was done about reducing the rent. People's grievance was that they were paying the highest rent of any township — for houses that were not worth it. The houses are three bedrooms, kitchen, living room, toilet and bathroom. They are one brick structure, no flooring and without ceiling. There is no geyser. Tenants must plaster the inside walls to cover the unsightly mazista bricks. They have to close the gaps on the asbestos roofing, and put up the ceiling. There is no guarantee that occupants will be reimbursed for expenses incurred to make the houses habitable. And yet in terms of the law the landlord must make sure that a house is habitable before tenants can move in.

People paid the provisional rent for four years. During that time they made the houses habitable. There was much discontent, particularly since those who tried to buy their homes were told they were overvalued. The Soweto Council was wanting R11 000 to R13 000, but building societies would not give loans, saying the houses' value was R6 000. Representation was made to the Soweto Council to no avail. The residents gave the council an ultimatum to review the rent or they would stop paying. They told the councillors that they were prepared to compromise by letting them treat the money they had been robbed of as deposit towards buying the homes. But all that fell on deaf ears and in March 1986, Chiawello 3 residents stopped paying rent.

Two months later the rest of Soweto did the same thing, although for different reasons.

It was a crucial time. Street committees were being formed, students were boycotting classes, and "necklacing" was common. Council police as well as councillors were being attacked. In Chiawello 3 for instance, a constable who was notorious for his sadistic raiding methods had his house gutted by fire. The fear of God came to constables and the councillors as well. House raids came to a stop. Councillors fled from Soweto and took refuge in town. The Council police (blackjacks) were suddenly seen moving about the township with rifles. A strange phenomenon in that not even the much feared SAP carry rifles. Only soldiers display rifles.

The months that followed were confusing. Rumours spread like fire — that payments would be credited towards home-ownership; that rent would be reduced; that evictions were coming; that other townships were paying rents secretly. In some areas refuse was not collected, and water and electricity came on and off. Some people said we could rest easy, because the government would do nothing to us until they had dealt with the Vaal boycott, which was three years older.

The Chiawello 3 issue was now part of the greater Soweto boycott. Some elements were for dialogue with the Soweto Council, but the day was won by those who refused to recognise the Councillors, saying they were placed by the government and not elected by the people. Another school would not hear of paying rent until Mandela and other political prisoners were released. A large part of their argument was that black people had no other means of communicating.

To some people this was downright stupid. They did not understand what rent had to do with politics. The proponents of the boycott said: "Was the creation of Soweto not politics? Where else could you find a landlord renting a house that is a health hazard and not being hurled to court? Where in the world do you find the landlord being the government? Where except in South Africa would you find that pertaining only to one section of its community? Where else would one find the security forces deployed to deal with rent defaulters?"

On 27 August 1986, White City residents clashed with municipal police and the army; 27 people died. Again, stories circulated like wildfire. Many said that armed ANC cadres had ambushed the police. Some said that local youths had been warned that evictions were to take place, and had prepared caches of stones to fight.

A few months later, the scene was almost repeated in Phomolong. Someone blew the "help" whistle and out came innocent tenants, thinking it was a genuine cry. Four died that night.

Came 1987, there was still uncertainty. People started to receive electricity and water bills only, with no rent statements. Evictions increased. There would be new rumours every few weeks, about different townships — now Emndeni, now Naledi, now Zola. At that point, street committees were no longer functioning, because leaders had been detained. There was no longer any co-ordination between the people and the comrades. People ceased to think in terms of street committees, and one by one, they started paying. No-one would publicly admit to be paying rent, but it was obvious that many were. People gave all sorts of excuses for being seen at the offices.

61

Some people paid so as to get taxi licences. "When I went for my licence they wanted my current latest rent receipt. I had to pay." Others paid when they went for permits to build on to their homes. Acquiring the 99-year lease also required up-to-date payment.

Chiawello residents received letters informing them that the rent issue was under review and tenants would be hearing from the council soon. This gave residents hope. But nothing more happened. People did not know how much they were owing. Main roads acquired bill-boards which even to this day still read: "water is a bargain, but even bargains must be paid for." The same was said of electricity, housing and transport. The inference was that residents do not want to pay, while what we want is to solve the problem so that we can pay. The houses appearing on the advert are, strangely enough, not the rented four-roomed structures, but the new development houses found in exclusive parts.

People became angry about the "bargain" advertisements, because water and electricity bills are astronomical. They are much higher than white homes, and the story is that we pay more per unit because the white areas have already paid off their infrastructure.

Besides, since the riots started in 1985 there has been no meter reader. How do they arrive at the figures? An average bill reads from R150 to R200. As for saying a rickety and dirty PUTCO bus is a bargain, that is beyond imagination. In Chiawello a taxi to town costs 10 cents less than a bus.

Came 1988, we welcomed the year with hope. People prayed the rent issue would be resolved. Then the Soweto Council started cracking the whip. They evicted people in certain areas of Chiawello 1 and 2, most of whom were pensioners. One was left out in the cold for the night and has since died of the exposure. Then one bright summer morning in Chiawello 3, residents were rudely awoken. There was a contingent. They wanted rent.

The soldiers stood pointing their rifles while officials demanded the current receipt. People mumbled a promise and were told that the soldiers would be back the following Thursday and woe betide defaulters.

Some residents rushed to pay or make a pledge to pay. Came the fateful Thursday and the officials kept their promise. Those who had not paid, had their furniture taken to the Superintendent's office. By evening there was chaos. The township was divided. Some had paid, some wanted to pay but had no money, some demanded solidarity in the name of the original Chiawello issue. Others demanded solidarity in the name of the big political issue.

Meetings were called. One went off well in the sense that it did take place although nothing came out of it. The next was disrupted by the arrival of the police who demanded a letter from the Commissioner of Police giving permission to hold the meeting.

Ultimately, a group of women marched to the Soweto Council chambers where they confronted the housing officer Miss Estelle Bester. She uncompromisingly told them unless the residents paid rent, including backlog, they would be in the street.

There is confusion unheard of in most townships of Soweto. But none is as bad as Chiawello 3. They have not achieved anything from the boycott. Instead they have a huge backlog to pay. The various committees that were set up have folded as people voted no-confidence in them. Every evening spells nightmare for some. Others have removed important and expensive pieces of furniture. Some have not recovered some of the items taken away, even after paying.

The leaders are behind bars or saying nothing. A few cases are with lawyers. The rest of the people wait for their fate to be decided, by the superintendents, the town clerk Nico Malan, the housing officer Ms Bester, the mayor Mr Botile and the councillors. They are Pontius Pilate in this matter.

11

Tato's funeral

———————— APRIL 1988 ————————

I HAVE been to many funerals. I have been to those where on re turning from the graveyard, I have thrown myself on my bed, drained. I have been to some where I was merely performing a duty, and to others simply to satisfy curiosity, as though to say: "Is he really dead," or "what will the funeral be like?" I have also been lured into attending funerals. What do you do when you visit a sister only to find she is on her way to a funeral of a person you hardly know? She persuades you to go along by sermonising "One day you will be dead and people won't come to your funeral." Who cares? I will be too dead to care, but I go with her anyway.

There are other ways of being hi-jacked to funerals. During the 1976 uprisings, students used to force motorists to drive them to the cemeteries to bury their comrades. Looking back, that was nothing compared to what happened ten years later. Then you were no longer made to go to the funeral but you did not expect to see your car again. You would be left at the roadside watching your car disappear into the distance with a driver working out the difference between brake and clutch and twenty shouting passengers.

I have just buried Tato. And yet I don't feel like I am from a funeral. Not that there was no solemn hymn singing and the usual "ashes to ashes" bit. No. Everything was there. Hearse, cortege, wreaths, artificial green grass where the chief mourners are to sit by the graveside, Soweto's who's who, and to crown it all, three dignified bishops of The True Church of Christ in Zion of South Africa in Soweto. They led the procession in their flowing maroon and black silk gowns. They took turns in preaching. This was done very demonstratively, the voices changing gears as the spirit moved them, climaxed by interjections of a long sonorous A—M—E—N.

And yet I still do not feel I have been to a funeral. This is in spite of the whole confusion and the rowdy business. On one side the ethereal angelic Catholics or Anglicans who are hushly doing their thing. On another side the Salvation Army's Christian Soldiers' brass band deafens us all. On the third side is an indigenous traditional congregation whose big women shriek heaven high adding new notes to the total distortion of John Wesley's creation, while their baritone backup of heavily bearded guys lends dignity to the occasion. Shovels at work here, the last post being played there. A siren pierces through the commotion, announcing the arrival of yet another funeral. People hurry to their cars. Those who manage to make it to the gates first leave gales of red dust behind as testimony of a job done and the need to get away. Bus drivers rev impatiently while passengers scramble for seats. Township funerals.

So Tato is dead. It is not that I do not believe it. However, I cannot come to grips with it. I can imagine him laughing at a shebeen as we talk of his funeral. He would certainly be the first to laugh at his lifeless body in the coffin. Tato, kawufane ucinge — just imagine, Tato dead.

At the graveside, when it was time for the body to descend to its final resting place — until the sound of the trumpet shall ring for all — the coffin would not go down. The poor undertaker's face was marked with beads of sweat. He did not know what to do. He kept fidgeting with the button controlling the lever to pull the coffin. Soon he had to abandon the fancy modern gadget and resort to the good old-fashioned ropes that he had to fetch from the car, leaving the coffin lying suspended in midair.

We had all thought it was a technical problem until someone remarked, "Trust Tato to refuse to go down without a fuss." People chuckled. But then another one was quick to say, "No, you are missing the point, kid, you forget that Tato had no time for old spinsters. He wouldn't go down on a hymn initiated by old Miss Pooe."

Now that made sense. During the tension as the coffin refused to go down and the African sun competed with the demands of dignity, singing had stopped. Lerna Horne, a well-known lady with a remarkable voice, saved the day. She started singing the popular funeral hymn Jerusalema e motsha (The new Jerusalem). By the time the undertaker came back with the ropes there was a roaring congregation. In no time, Tato was out of sight, down there. He probably waved us goodbye as he descended to his last place of abode, as they say.

Tato also loathed teetotallers. Once at a friend's funeral vigil, a drunk took the floor. He was supposed to give tribute to the deceased. Instead, he went on a long sob story about himself saying things such as "I have really lost a friend. I wonder with whom shall I share my nip of brandy now that Masondo is dead." He went on and on, much to the embarrassment of the audience and annoyance of the master of ceremonies who stopped him short: "Thank you brother, that will be enough, please sit down. This is no place for drunks." Tato saw red. He stood up and demanded, "What right have you to belittle my friend when he is expressing his feelings about someone he knew and loved. You, who can hardly lift an empty beer glass. What do you know about the deceased? And as for you" he turned pointing to the man who had sat down, "you shall never have another opportunity to give praise to our friend. Come and say your piece."

The man stood up and continued with his speech as though nothing had happened. He went on to say, "I envy his wife Mampinga who will soon get a man to share the huge double bed and the long cold nights with" and sat down sobbing profusely. He was escorted out of the tent and given a stiff tot of brandy.

I met Tato many years ago at a wedding. There was this immaculate man at our table dressed in old-style formality. His well trimmed grey hair set like a halo on a face that bore lines of wisdom. We had just finished eating the usual sumptuous wedding luncheon when Tato said to the man next to him: "My friend, I am not in the habit of eating and moving off without thanking my host." Standing up and fixing his out-dated tuxedo and clearing his moustache of crumbs, he moved to the bridal table.

"Manene Namanenekazi, ndiyabulela kwaba bantwana ude bafike kulomgangatho onina noyise abangakhange bafunyelele kuwo." He shook hand with the couple and walked away leaving the guests roaring with laughter.

Apparently both the groom and the bride were children born out of wedlock. Both pairs of parents had never got round to getting married. So Tato had congratulated the couple for doing better than their parents.

After he had left, I was among the many who wanted to know who the witty old man was and the answer we got was, he was Tata Mthimkulu, generally known as Tato.

I was later to meet him at all sorts of places. I would collide with him at funerals, political rallies, soccer matches, shebeens, almost everywhere, and always he was the jolly old man with a bag full of funny stories.

He professed to know everybody. He claimed to have been in the ANC when it was formed, the PAC when it broke off from the ANC and BCM when it was started. Can you believe that? Who wouldn't believe Tato once he started talking. In most cases it wasn't so much believing what he said but being mesmerised with the manner in which he spoke.

He would make fun of everybody, even himself. One of the best shows he put up was when imitating Potlako Leballo of the PAC smoking a tobacco-less pipe at the old Synagogue in Pretoria during the Great Treason Trial. Who were we to argue with him when we hardly knew the people? So he was our mirror to our heroes.

In his style he would brag and tell us how he's brushed shoulders with so-and-so, people we only read in history books. Of course he was on first name terms with them all.

Another masterpiece was his narration of his wedding night. "And there was Mamtolo huddled up in the corner with her big eyes as though about to fall off." He would emit a hearty laugh. "Seeing her coiled up like an embryo I lost my temper and said 'hlala kahle man, andina kutya'." (Sit properly man, I am not about to eat you up.) If anybody asked him why he was angry with a young scared girl from the homelands thrust into an arranged marriage with a man twice her senior, he said "that night in particular I was in no mood for a virgin." Although Tato had come to Johannesburg at a very tender age and had practically grown up in the city, when it came to choosing a wife, his parents had organised a bride for him. So he was torn between maintaining tradition and forfeiting his township lovers. Nor was it any better for the girl. She was to spend the rest of her life with this man who was a stranger to her as well as acclimatise to township life.

Tato got along with everybody. He seemed to have an understanding for all people. "My boy, never play around with a tsotsi. Tsotsis have no scruples" was one of his bits of advice. He would then tell his favourite tsotsi/mfundisi joke. The story was of a punter pastor, who borrowed money from a tsotsi on a hot tip. But something slipped up and his horse did not come in. The pastor could not meet his obligation towards the tsotsi.

"On the Sunday he should have paid the tsotsi," narrated Tato, "Mfundisi preached on Jesus' entry to Jerusalem, how he commanded his disciples to get him a donkey. Meanwhile from the pulpit he could see through the window. The tsotsi was standing outside with a knife, gesticulating to him demanding his money.

"With his hands in the air, the pastor said 'Jesus did not have means of transport. Bazalwane, when someone says he does not have, he means just that. And people must understand. I mean, I don't have. Understand.'

"Outside the tsotsi could hear every word said inside. He pointed the knife in the direction of the pastor who got the message and said 'Nhlanganiso enhle [good congregation] I shall now have the collection and conclude as I have somewhere to go lest you attend my funeral'. Somehow the tsotsi got his money back."

Tato never went to church. His reason: "I do not want to go to heaven when I die, fancy meeting Ou Strydom, Smuts, Malan, Verwoerd and who's the ancestor of the boers? Ja, the great pirate Ou Jan van Riebeeck and his fancy hairdo.

"What if I should find there is separate development out there? No. I want to go down there and meet my ancestors. The guy I really am looking forward to meeting to iron out a few things with is Shaka. Boy, if only he'd lived longer, we'd be talking of a different South Africa. I'd be some roving Foreign Affairs minister confusing everybody wherever I go.

"I'd also like to meet the great Moshoeshoe and congratulate him on his stone-throwing techniques. Heaven knows where Leabua Jonathan would be if Moshoeshoe had not gone up Thaba Bosiu and kept rolling them down. Jonathan would still be down there in the pits of the earth singing *Abelungu, ngo damn, basibiza ngo Jim*. Today he sits pretty well.

"I'd meet the mothers of Africa. I will have quite a time getting to know them.

"And if you ask me what shall I tell them on where I come from, I do not have the answer. Shall I tell them that we are busy wasting time splitting hairs over nothing, killing each other for no reason?" Each time he spoke like that, clouds would gather in his eyes and even those who tend to laugh over nothing knew that Tato had entered another plane.

"What has happened to us? Why are we killing each other so much? Look at the witchhunting and the backbiting that is happening all around us? Why can't we sit down and talk of the problems instead of destroying each other. No," he would say, shaking his head as though talking to himself. Maybe he was. "The fault is not with us. We are but pawns in the game. Where in the world have you seen a nation that has been denied its leaders like we have? All the nations in the world have people they look up to but us. Even animals have the lion to look up to. What do we have?

"What happens to children in a home without parents? Why are we expected to be different? Everyone is faced with his or her day-to-day struggle and the larger struggle is meant to take care of itself. Is there any wonder we are tearing each other up the way we do?"

On such occasions, Tato would leave unceremoniously and those who knew him grew to appreciate not to bother him.

Tato was very crude in dishing out what he regarded as advice. His nephew told him he had been offered a better job but could not bring himself to resign and leave his employer in the lurch. Tato hit the roof.

"From today, you must stop telling people that you are my relation," he screamed. "I don't even want to know you. Get out of my sight. You disgust me.

"Fancy feeling sorry for leaving your baas. When will black people ever be liberated, nnxh," emitting air from the back part of his half empty gums. "Do they ever feel sorry for you when they fire you?

"I used to know real liberated guys. For instance there was this guy who went to a Portuguese shop to buy some tobacco. 'Yes can I help you' asked the grimy looking Porto. But before he could reply, in walked a thick-set boer. The Porto immediately forgot all about the black guy and attended to the boer. Then when he returned to him he said, 'Sorry my friend, by the way what was your order?'

"Oh, me," he said. From his backpocket he took out a wad of bank notes and made as if he was counting up.

"Can I have 18 packets of fish and chips. Hot please."

"18 fish and mazambane" shouted the Portuguese to the kitchen staff.

"Can I have 18 loaves of white bread, cut into thin slices please and 18 pieces of cheese put into the fish and chips."

"No, my friend," advised the Portuguese, now very respectful. "It's going to be hot and messy. Make them separate, heh?"

"Hey wena", shouted the shopowner to the kitchen staff. "Hurry, the gentleman is in a big hurry. Chop-chop."

A black woman emerged from the kitchen carrying a huge box full of goodies.

"Is that all my friend?" asked the Portuguese, sorting out the food and adding up.

"No," said the black guy. "Do you have Hungarian goulash?"

"What?" said the Porto. "Eh, no, no, not today," rubbing his hands and smiling.

"Well, if you don't have Hungarian goulash I can't have that food. Sorry," and dashed out of the shop before the Portuguese could fish his gun from below the counter.

The coffin went down, down. A thousand questions flashed in my mind. Soon it was over. People rushed to the cars. My knees could not carry me. A candle that had illuminated Soweto had been blown out. Soon it would be dark and I would get lost in the midst of it all. I wondered who could see the way?

All around I could see bright smiling faces, and yet none knew happiness. It was all a veneer. Beneath, people actually feared searching for the truth.

I looked at the roads ahead of me. I knew all the roads led to the winning post, or so we all thought. Yet I could not find one I felt was taking us there.

That night, as I lay in my bed, I realised how sometimes a child is born, grows up to shine among people. Eventually when it dies it leaves a trail of blessings to those who have been fortunate enough to come closer to it. And even that, makes life worth the pain.

12

Appointment with the hangman

———— APRIL/MAY 1988 ————

*Written on the day before the
scheduled execution of six people*

THEY say hope springs eternal in the human breast and that where there is life there is hope. For relatives of condemned people, these are not jokes. From the moment the judge pronounces the death sentence, those involved will carry the fear and anxiety like an invisible cross. They will spend the rest of their lives asking questions such as: "Was he really hanged?" or "Is it true that they are kept somewhere in the bowels of the earth minting money?" (There are strong rumours in black circles that people are not hanged but are incarcerated in some building in Pretoria making money. This myth is strengthened by the claims that there hasn't been anybody coming out of the black community who has actually professed to be working or having worked in a minting factory) or, "Why are we never shown the bodies?"

After the initial shock of the sentence and the mother or wife has recovered, these women will temporarily wipe the tears, pick up their skirts and move heaven and earth to save their dear ones from the gallows. Once more, lawyers are consulted. Special prayers are held. Inyangas are consulted. No stone is left unturned. The next shock to be suffered is when the date of the hanging is announced. The judge's words drum through your head.

The worst of all days is the day before the hanging.

Death is a mystery. Although we live in the shadow of death, somehow we never get used to it. One may have a very sick relative and be reconciled to the fact that he may be dying any minute. But when that minute comes, the very people who had accepted the

71

inevitable reject the reality. Accepting hanging is difficult. The fact that one may die of choking from food or from a motor car accident is one thing. Knowing that someone somewhere is a special person who lives among people, a father, perhaps a lover, maybe a warm-natured person, a respectable citizen, who stops for old ladies to pass, never says anything untoward to anybody, and that person is the one who turns the switch that severs life from a person, is even harder to reconcile. Since the issue lies in the hands of someone with power, somehow the victim and all those involved nurse the hope until the last minute that there might just be a change of heart from the people who wield power. I saw an old woman of 70 who had been a Christian all her life lose faith and belief in the Almighty because of a son who was executed. She came out of the chapel after being shown coffins and being told that one of them held her son's remains. "Fancy for the preacher to lie to us and say our children have been called by God when they have killed them in front of us. Only a white God does that."

The eve before the hanging is the most cruel day for those visiting Pretoria maximum prison. That day, all concerned try by all means to visit their dear ones. People will be coming from all over the country. There will be some from as far as Cape Town and Zululand who may be spending the night at the prison. There are waiting-cum-sleeping rooms for those without accommodation at neighbouring townships. There are usually one or two whites to hang and a host of blacks, the place is always swarming with black, Indian and coloured people. It is not possible to see condemned white people because, true to South African tradition, their cells are removed. One wonders if they use different coloured people as hangmen.

The large double doors open with the clang of metal. Behind the screen are huge men in blue uniforms. Someone once remarked that there is nowhere else where one finds boers as big as the ones at Pretoria Central. Tall, hefty, with blue eyes. They give visitors long cold stares while asking for the name of the prisoner and let you through. Security is so tight, they never bother to ask for visitors' particulars. There is nothing a visitor could do to let anybody escape once he is in there.

You walk along the peaceful long passage in one of the cleanest prisons in South Africa. Maybe in the whole of the continent. There are broad tarred lanes where sometimes one can see a contingent of black men with shining heads in prisoners' clothes going through the exercises.

Out there your eyes are also enchanted by well-manicured sprawling lawns and flowers. No one watches over you but the feeling of being watched is with you all the time. As you walk in that corridor of death, you make a silent prayer that none of the remaining dear ones ever give you cause to have to come here. You want to turn back and lecture to your son and all your nephews. You will do that later. For now, you have to be strong and face the one to be hanged.

There is nobody to escort visitors. Somehow, you follow the crowd. After all there is only one reason you are all here. There is no rush here. Talking is in subdued tones. Others drift along like zombies up to the visitors' reception area. The most human black policemen are to be found here. They are the first to greet visitors, sometimes even ask after your health. They don't seem to have grown used to anguish. They are important people because tradition has it that on the eve of hanging, the one to hang the next day offers sweets to those remaining. The policemen are the ones who buy the sweets from the money left as gifts for the prisoners.

There is a step of hope. Hope that something drastic may happen. But as one enters the room and takes a place at one of the windows, one is enveloped by the great fear that it is your brother, sister, husband, friend's last day on earth. You wrestle with hope against hope that maybe it is not. You ask yourself the question "What do I say to him". You stand by the window next to the microphone while he is being called. Next to you a conversation might be in progress between a relative and a condemned person. You are able to hear all they are saying. Soon yours will emerge from the passage in front of where you are standing. He will be a picture of health. Remember they are fed well and they are not worked. He will be clean shaven in immaculate khaki shirt and shorts. He may be carrying a bible.

Your eyes will meet and you will look down, perhaps to stop a tear or trying not to let him see that you are about to cry. Maybe at that stage he may start a familiar hymn and fellow prisoners join in and the whole place becomes a church. Someone preaches.

It's amazing how much of a blanket worshipping becomes. With everyone desperately trying not to crack, they all cling to the flimsy invisible anchor of Christianity.

There will be those who will be overcome by emotions and let the tears stream down the cheeks. Some will go faint and be carried outside. There is no screaming. Those to hang may be musing or speaking softly to relatives giving last minute instructions on what to be done after he has been executed. If he is a father he will ask after the children who are under-age, who are not allowed to visit prisons. And perhaps his wife may have brought pictures of the children and show them to him through the glass barrier. He will then tell his wife to look after the children, ask her to make sure

73

they go to church and to school. One by one, relatives and friends will go to the window and have something to say to him. At this stage, the prisoners are on another plane. They have made peace with their creator and are telling visitors how they are looking forward to meeting him. They console their dear ones and tell them to be brave and wait for the day when they'll meet. They all have smiling faces, perhaps dancing and singing to the hymns.

These may have been murderers, rapists or guerillas. But before the crowd then, they are loved ones whom they will be seeing for the last time that morning or afternoon. Beneath that veneer of Christianity, of bravery, of anxiety to meet one's God, there is still hope. Hope that the lawyers may pull out a card. Hope that some sudden new evidence may prove one's innocence. Hope that somewhere people in power may just have a re-think.

Beneath that veneer one asks all sorts of questions. Just as one is asking questions today as the Sharpeville Six wait for tomorrow's appointment with the hangman. How a judge can sentence people to death on circumstantial evidence? How one can be executed for being part of the crowd? How many more such deaths before this country wakes up to realising that capital punishment will not bring peace? That jails will not stop people from demanding their rights as citizens? The fact that the six will meet the hangman simply because someone said they were there makes me shudder.

I have lived with all sorts of violence. I was once attacked by a group of 10 or 12 men and watched helplessly as they looted food, clothing and money from my house. I was lucky not to have been raped or maimed. My children had to live through that ordeal. I have seen a person being stabbed and die before my helpless eyes.

I have seen a political mob at work, and I have seen people being dragged into actions they would not like to have done. I have seen 12-year-olds threaten old and helpless people.

During the first months of the rent boycott, I listened to an old woman narrate how youngsters harassed her the entire evening for having paid her rent. They broke every glass and furniture in her house, playing trampoline on her sofa and bed.

I once watched 15-year-olds beat up a girl of 12 whose crime had been to go to school when a boycott was on. They made a bonfire of her books and her uniform. She was released to go home in her panties. I know teenagers who were collected from homes for meetings to discuss the struggle. What do you do when you are told to necklace an informer, and refusing implies you are condoning "sell-outs" and therefore your home will be gutted? How many strong men have surrendered the keys to their vehicles at the threats from children?

How many youngsters languish in prison for crimes they did not do? Victims of informers who had run out of stories, victims of petty jealousies and witch-hunting. It could have been my daughter or son seen with the mob and someone decided to tell the cops. I shudder.

At the height of "comrade mania", my sister was stopped by youths for driving a "target", meaning a car belonging to a white company. It was forcefully taken away from her and she had to find her way home.

Later, she was subpoenaed. At court, she was surprised to be shown a strange boy as the one who had taken the car. She told the prosecutor she had never seen the accused before. No amount of persuasion (friendly or otherwise) from the prosecutor could make her say different. The boy was acquitted. It turned out later that the boy had nothing to do with the youths who had terrorised my sister. In fact, they had decided to nail him with the crime because he had resisted joining them.

In 1976 when the security police were detaining students, they visited the home of an activist in a street where I used to live. When they got to the boy's home, his mother denied she had a son with that name. She said the Vusi they were looking for lived at house number such-and-such, down the road. When the police got to that house no questions were asked. The poor boy was bungled into the van and spent over 18 months in prison. He is now 27 years old, suffers from high blood pressure, without matric and without a job. A bitter man.

We know the story of the Soweto Eleven who paid for the crimes that took place during 1976. We know that there was no evidence against them except for the fact that they were the student leaders. There was not a single witness who saw any of the eleven lift a stone to cause anybody any harm. Nor was there a witness who saw any one of the eleven set any building alight. They were guilty of being leaders and of addressing meetings which, the court alleged, incited the students to go on a rampage. They spent two years awaiting trial. Some were acquitted while others were given a jail sentence. That, unfortunately, is justice according to whites in South Africa.

For as long as blacks are not part of the governing body, and as long as the law is designed by whites, without blacks and the judiciary displays insensitivity as has been happening lately, and as long as white soldiers can, because of Botha's protection, get away with crimes such as the killing of innocent civilians in Namibia, while black rioters are sent to the gallows on flimsy or no evidence, then hope and security for this country will remain a pipe dream.

Instead we are sure to see more blacks going to Pretoria Maximum Prison either as visitors or to keep the appointment with the hangman.

13

Queries over creativity

WRITER Mbulelo Mzamane speaks of the 50's as the golden years. It was a time when, in spite of the government, black people seemed to be in full bloom. Out of the townships came plays such as King Kong, Spono and Emperor Jones. There were songbirds such as Miriam Makeba and Dolly Rathebe as well as crooners of the likes of Nathan Dambuza Mdledle of the Manhattan Brothers, Caiphus Semenya and many others. There were writers such as Can Themba, E'skia Mphahlele, Nat Nakasa and Henry Nxumalo.

The new musical King Afrika shows the level to which black life has sunk. If writers can no longer pen inspiring work and if songwriters can no longer raise the masses from the depression, society is in danger.

Look back at King Kong. Here we had black and white writers who came together to write a story about a black boxer in the ghetto. Nothing phoney. The likes of Todd Matshikiza as well as white writers produced the play. The township scenes were convincing, and so was the acting. It had its flaws but on the whole it was a historic event.

Thirty years later another musical hits the scene — King Afrika, also about a boxer. It would appear the writer did not think issues through. For instance the wife appears in dashing western African dress combined with traditional Zulu head-gear. I find this ridiculous. It shows that the writers are not in touch. They know nothing about Zulus, except as a glamorous image, and one wonders why the Zulus involved in the show do not enlighten them.

The so-called traditional Zulu woman does not wear dresses. The Zulus and the Swazis do not have what one would call a traditional dress. They use a very short pleated skirt made out of skin. In fact when leather hit the South African fashion, Zulus used to call those who went crazy about leather "Johnny come late" because they had long ago been wearing garments made out of skin — the bheshu, the skirt (isidwaba), the underpants (iqoyi), head-gear (ungiyane).

Came the Europeans and cloth, Zulu maidens took to wraps and towels. However, the older women wear vests or t-shirts over isidwaba and use two to three wraps or towels. And you don't have to go to Zululand to see that. Zulu maidens can be seen braving the Transvaal cold air in towelling that goes as far as the knees. For a research in Zulu women's traditional dress, a trip to Westgate station would suffice. There you could feed your eyes on the hair-dos, the wraps and the beads, as the women bend over the braziers selling offal, mealies and trotters.

Abigail Kubheka's role was questionable as one did not know if she was the mother-in-law or what. One would have expected that as an old horse at this game she should have been better cast. At one stage she was in high-heeled shoes, fancy trousers and Zulu head-gear. What a sight. Maybe the futuristic Zulu outfit. When it came to Henry Cele, I could only think that here was liberal work at play. The casting of Cele endorsed the much spoken-about black leaders syndrome.

Certain leaders have been imposed by white liberals on the masses. These leaders are quoted in the media, address white groups in town and are photographed in white society. But if you stop to check you are sad to discover in their own localities they are unknown. The same goes for some actors. Looking at Cele in Shaka Zulu one can condone his acting there, in a stately and majestic role. There he did not have to prance like boxers do. Remember there was a time when all black boys were going to be boxers until Kung-Fu hit the scene. We can recognise boxers, they walk with a distinctive swaggering deportment. But Cele plodded about in a way no black would relate to a boxer.

I had no quarrel with the white dancers. Not being schooled in white dancing I have nothing to say about them. But I do want to know what the significance of their being there was. Is it to project the kind of Africa we would like to see? Sounds like normal dancing in an abnormal society to me.

But I do have something to say about the black dancing. Even Savuka with his white skin would have shamed them. When a Zulu warrior picks his leg up in dance, the entire body is involved. It is forceful, yet graceful. For Zulu boys dancing is not just an act, it is spiritual. We do get a bit of that in Savuka when he does serious dancing before he gets on to the political progressive-language business. But here we had alleged Zulus dancing as if a ballet-teacher had choreographed it.

The less said about the female dancers the better. Theirs is a worse version of "Iphi-Ntombi", where black girls gyrate and wriggle their bums and thighs to the white old men's joy. Nothing African about the dance, commercial erotic dance.

As for the lyrics, they are so unAfrican. In fact, considering the kind of persons whom we were told were assisting in this production one gets terribly disappointed.

I wondered what the writers were saying to us black people. King Afrika rose from nothing to be a champ, and suddenly stumbled, fell and lost his dream. From there we suddenly hear something about a bright future for all. Is that to say to us that never mind the many times that we fall, we should not harbour bitterness. That we must remain happy no matter what?

If the writers are so concerned about a better future, they do not tell us how that future can come about. Are they talking of a better future in the present system? Are they implying that this is possible?

They say writers and artists always reflect the truth of their times. When it comes to King Afrika, I find it sad that the story of the African does not change. It is the same old theme, Jim Comes to Jo'burg. When blacks put up a show it is about township life. Yet when whites write black plays it is usually about rural black life. The subject of blacks moving out of the homelands and being confronted by the city fascinates the white writers.

They have not yet begun to see us as we see ourselves. My children for instance, have no desire to visit Nongoma or Bogum. They do not relate to those towns. They never stop to remind me that people who live there are my relatives not theirs. Many people seen walking in Jo'burg were born in Sophiatown, Newclare or Albertville.

I used to be amused by an old liberal who was fond of saying: "The happy black man is the one who sits outside his hut, drinking his bantu beer watching his wives work while the umfaan looks after the cattle." I do not know where he got that scene from. Whether it is once more what white artists paint or is his imagination running wild. Only a migrant worker on holiday can afford to have cattle and the wives rushing in and out cooking. Otherwise it is a pathetic scene. The man might have been employed at some stage of his life, now he is back home probably suffering from tuberculosis and the many children running around are kwashiorkor cases. I am surprised the actors are surprised that the black community feels King Afrika is another Info song. Can you blame them when they see black and whites singing together in jollity and you hear lyrics such as "Ikusasa eliqhakazile" or some such Info line.

14

Where only police disturb the calm

TOURIST postcards show brightly painted houses and smiling Ndebele women with beaded necklaces. But the real life of Ndebele people has become dominated by something which will never be seen in postcards — a police force called Imbokodo.

"Imbokodo" is an ancient word for a stone used for crushing and grinding. It has taken a new meaning in KwaNdebele.

For years, KwaNdebele was dominated by two chiefs — Mapogo Nzuza Mahlangu and Mabhena Manana. Mapogo enjoys the status of supreme chief. Both chiefs live in the remote areas of KwaNdebele, Nzuza in Vaalfontein and Mabhena at Allemansdrift.

When Pretoria decided that the Ndebele people wanted "homeland" status, instead of looking among the two families for a leader, the bureaucrats eased a businessman, Simon Skosana, into the office of Chief Minister. Skosana organised vigilantes to grind and crush all that stood in his way. They called themselves the Mbokodo.

Now, the fear of Mbokodo is the dominant feature in KwaNdebele villages. If you travel in any part of KwaNdebele you notice the unwillingness of the people to talk. This is coupled with the stares one gets. This is a small community and visitors stick out prominently. At all the villages, people share the fear of Mbokodo and allegiance to Chief Mapogo.

They say that Majozi, the new Chief Minister Mr George Mahlangu, usurped power from his mentor Chief Mapogo. In their minds, Majozi studied Mapogo's secrets so as to torpedo him. "James should have taken over, not Majozi" is what most Ndebele people say.

Perhaps if Majozi had not been raised by Mapogo, there would be less animosity and bitterness. The story told by everyone is that George was a fatherless boy who was raised by Chief Mapogo. They shared the same surname. Mapogo Mahlangu of the Mgwezani clan and George Mahlangu of the Dima clan.

George was raised with Mapogo's sons, Cornelius and James. "As youngsters, Majozi was closer to James. They grew up together, playing alongside and went to the University of Ngoye about the same time," said one woman. When I first got to KwaNdebele one of the women kept making reference to the king and I asked if she meant the Chief Minister. She raised her nose and frowned: "Majozi is no king; not that rascal." I later learned this view is universal. People say that Majozi has two criminal charges outstanding against him.

Traditionalists

The Ndebele people are traditionalists. They cling with unusual tightness to their traditions. For instance extended families are a common feature. Among other groups the traditional extended family is fading, but with the Ndebele it is strong as ever. With a quarter of the population sharing the Mahlangu, Skosana, Manana or Mabhena surnames, one finds the entire nation to be composed of relatives. And on top of that, is the fact that young and able-bodied people live away from home for long periods. Thus the old people continue to be important in the community and the traditions stay alive. This is the reverse of what happens in the urban townships where the old people are rendered irrelevant and now there is even talk of old-age homes.

Of all black groups, the Ndebeles are the least educated. For a person from Soweto or from Zululand to go to KwaNdebele is like going to a past time. A symptom is the way people count money in pounds. Flush toilets are unknown to many.

In town you can see clusters of Ndebele people blocking the pavement. They walk together in a colourful bunch. When they are faced with a lift in a building that is another story. They are petrified. There is great jostling and pulling-in and pulling-out.

For the women, life means raising the children and running the home while men work in the city. The menfolk usually have humble jobs and live in hostels in the city.

They are humble people who don't know if they have rights which can be protected. Few dare to bring legal suits against the Mbokodo. When questioned they answer "Mbokodo deals with the whites and who dare question them?"

They use a lot of Afrikaans words such as *reg* for right and *skoni* for skoonsuster or some in-law person. Their main word for bad behaviour is *stront*.

The white man's word is final. They will not question anything a white person does. They say "Ikhuwa li reg" meaning the white man is right.

And yet for all their smiles and docility, they are like a rock opposing independence. This is not so much because they are aware of the implications of losing their South African citizenship, but because Mapogo and his sons are not leading.

Resistance

The story of KwaNdebele is one of the simplest stories in the history of homelands. For some years Pretoria played its game with Skosana. The people saw Skosana becoming prominent. They asked who was he and what was going on, but they were not really bothered. Then out of the blue they were called to a meeting and told KwaNdebele was to be independent on 4 November, 1985.

People were angry. They were being told of a big and mystifying new development by a person they barely respected. They asked what was their Chief saying. A mass meeting took place at the Chief's kraal and it was decided that independence was not wanted.

Even at this stage, people were not much concerned. But then Skosana started Mbokodo to suppress resistance, and from then the chaos began.

Mbokodo came down harshly, beating and detaining people. Majozi became the number two man in Mbokodo. People were being detained everywhere. No-one knew who was doing what to whom. The chief of Imbokodo, Enoch Ntuli, became widely feared.

Then Ntuli was killed by a car bomb. At about the same time, Majozi was detained. Many people thought one of the criminal cases against him had been reopened. But he was soon out and again with the Mbokodo. He succeeded Ntuli as chief of Mbokodo.

During the chaos, the shops owned by the cabinet ministers were burned. Many buildings were destroyed. To this day you see their shells everywhere. The Ministers went to a hide-out in Verena, a farm area near Bronkhorstspruit. Eventually the plans for independence were stopped. Then Skosana died of natural causes and Majozi was made Chief Minister. This made people suspicious because he had not been in the cabinet before and not even in parliament.

Casino rights

One cabinet member had been Prince Cornelius, Chief Mapogo's son. As Minister of Education, he would be seen zooming in and out of the villages in his large chauffeur-driven BMW. Young people used to make reference to the fact that he was a minister of education with a standard four certificate. He was able to acquire a large supermarket and a bottle store as well as four wives during his political term.

The story widely told is that Cornelius had at first tried to persuade his father to accept independence. It is said that he and Skosana and Skosana's son, Sam, had made some arrangements regarding the granting of casino rights. An independent KwaNdebele would be on the doorstep of Pretoria and close to Johannesburg. If a casino was built there, it would knock the bottom out of the Sun City market.

At the time the comrades were on the rise and the ministers were on the run, Prince Cornelius was called to a meeting by the anti-independence people. They were against the other ministers but they wanted to hear him out because he was Mapogo's son.

At that meeting, Cornelius humbled himself and apologised. He told the people that from that moment he was against independence. They forgave him and embraced him. His shops were not set alight. But Cornelius stayed in the cabinet. When Majozi became Chief Minister he excluded Cornelius from meetings for fear he would be eavesdropping for the people. Soon he was axed from parliament and later thrown in jail.

Meanwhile many people were saying that Prince James should be Chief Minister. Although younger than Cornelius, James is well educated, with a university degree. It would appear James was against independence from the start as would be expected of a graduate. Mind you, Majozi is also a graduate come to that.

Detentions

After a period on the defensive, Mbokodo rallied and reformed. It was now the vigilantes' turn to burn the shops which the youth onslaught had spared. Beatings and detentions flared up with new force. Chief Mapogo's house was attacked and gutted. James, Cornelius and Sam Skosana were thrown in jail and overnight became heroes, feted as leaders of the anti-homeland cause.

At this point, everybody rapidly became "politicised". A woman says: "Our children were not interested until the Mbokodo started assaulting their fathers and uncles. Now we have wholesale war."

Another woman said: "They go to any home and demand to speak to the boys. They wake us up in the dead of night and beat up or detain our sons indefinitely. This is done whether he is an activist or not. Majozi and his bandits (amabandiete) are like King Herod, they don't want male children in KwaNdebele."

The KwaNdebele government says that Mbokodo has been disbanded. People say that Mbokodo has been given uniforms and turned into Kitskonstabels. They recognise the same members. They maintain Imbokodo has been legalised. "When we questioned, the police told us anybody was free to join the police force," said a woman in Moutse.

Many women say that their sons have gone to the bush. There are stories of skirmishes, told in hushed tones.

People talk mainly about bread and butter issues like jobs and schooling.

"Look, I would rather we got independence than remain as poor as we are. Maybe we can get jobs and I would be able to come back from Johannesburg," said a man who was home on holiday.

But some nurses had different ideas. They said marasmas, pellagra and kwashiokor were severe as a result of homeland circumstances. "There are no shops in Vaalbank. They were burnt down by the comrades. People are dying of hunger.

"These are the people who were deported from Alexandra township. They were not even Ndebeles. Clerks looked at their surnames and decided they would belong to the KwaNdebele nation. They were first dumped at Kameelrivier, later taken to Allemansdrift, now to Vaalbank." They travel to Pretoria or the Reef for work. A return trip to Pretoria is R13,60.

Majozi protected

Siyabuswa, the first capital, is a large township with identical houses. In the centre are a few architecture buildings, one was the parliament. The only recreational centre of any sort is the Bundu Inn some distance off, mostly patronised by white salesmen doing their rounds.

The capital was moved from Siyabuswa to KwaMhlanga. Most people figure it out that the move was made to protect Majozi because Siyabuswa (meaning "we are ruled") was in the centre of a heavily populated area. KwaMhlanga is nearer Pretoria and is 15 kilometres away from the nearest village or township.

Nobody knows where KwaNdebele begins or ends. Some of it is in South Africa and other parts are inside BophuthaTswana. "We have had to accept women in labour who have been chased away by both governments from their clinics because they do not belong there," said a nurse.

Yet in spite of the atmosphere, children are at school. Adult education centres are supported by teachers and nurses trying to upgrade their qualifications. The teachers' training college next to Siyabuswa has students from urban townships. Strangely enough, there are many Soweto students schooling in KwaNdebele and they are not automatically accused of being troublemakers — contrary to the way they are treated in other homelands. In Dennilton the Catholic parish is a hive of activity from toddlers attending the creche to women working on crafts.

In the past, this society survived on subsistence farming, now they have patches of garden. The women can no longer plant "morogo" (spinach) which is their staple diet. They make crafts to sell in the cities.

"I could not survive without selling beadwork," said one old woman. She acts as a courier for others who cannot travel to Johannesburg. She collects their work and catches a truck ride. She does not charge for taking her neighbours' work with her.

Others buy vegetables in season and sell them in the townships. They are called "Abomkhozi" by township people. They travel in groups carrying grass brooms, fresh mealies and beans. They hire a truck to drive them to Johannesburg. They may stay in the township for about a week, until their wares are sold. They hire a room to share. They sleep huddled on the floor, using their goods as pillow. "We are afraid of Johannesburg tsotsis but then what can we do? That is where the money is."

They do not realise that the tsotsis are more afraid of them. Abomkhozi are never robbed. They are in no danger because of all people they are believed to have the most powerful muti. There is a saying that if you rob abomkhozi you must hold the sun to stop it from setting, because once it sets you will never see it rise again.

These women are a bunch of honest people. They will never steal a hairpin if they entered anybody's house in absentia. They will not charge you a cent extra or take money that is not theirs. If you owe one Mkhozi and ask one of her colleagues to pass on the money, you can rest assured it will be done.

Ndebele women are powerful even more than women elsewhere. The women are the main members of the family. They run the homes and they are the ones who know what is going on in Kwa-Ndebele. They attend the meetings and take the important decisions. And yet KwaNdebele is the only homeland which officially precludes women from voting.

Simple lives

Although there is nothing rural about KwaNdebele, people lead a very unsophisticated lifestyle. Except for brick houses owned by business people or a few missionaries, the homes are made of mud. Some villages have running water at street corners. In others there is just one tap, usually in a church yard.

But hooliganism and thuggery is unheard of. There are no faction fights in KwaNdebele. There are no witch-hunts or muti murders. You never hear of gruesome family violence or anything of that nature in KwaNdebele. People walk anywhere anytime in no fear of muggers. The only violence which they experience is from Mbokodo.

15

Friend in need

I WAS born in Soweto. This means I can never get lost in any part of Johannesburg, nor can I ever be mugged or taken for a ride. So I thought. Just as some healthy people never think they could one day suffer from cancer, I always thought only country bumpkins fall prey to muggers and charlatans who linger around street corners selling rings and watches.

Depending on where you are in Johannesburg, Saturday can be a boring day. I had spent some time in the quiet atmosphere of Braamfontein and when I drove home, I suddenly remembered I was to have dinner at a friend's place. My host being a dear old friend who has made a habit of showering me with gifts each time she has been abroad, I decide to buy her a hot-water bottle for her troublesome back. I turned left at Simmonds Street and headed for Hillbrow.

It was a beautiful autumn day. One of those days when you know that soon the amazing blue sky will give way to an endless sheet of dull grey blanket. Soon the unbearable sun, which we take so much for granted, would be something yearned for in the cold winter days approaching. A day whose warmth you savour till sunset. Although the birds above the trees where I was parking were not singing, there seemed to be a great deal of activity going on above me. Maybe they were packing their bags to leave for sunnier countries.

I felt good as I parked the car, placing my groceries out of sight so as not to attract would-be thieves. I checked if all the windows were shut and the doors locked. I put the car-keys into my bag, gave my back to the car and strode away, humming. I could not have been more content. Actually I appreciated the fact that I was out here all by myself, with none of my kids telling me how to spend my money. It was good to be healthy and alive.

I had taken about three steps when I felt something hit my arm very hard and I almost landed on the ground. For a few seconds I was in a daze. When I came to, my bag was gone.

At the corner of my mind I seemed to hear a voice saying: "Wake up, you have been mugged." I screamed: "Help!" Like a mad woman I gave chase while screaming in Sotho "Tshwarang!" meaning "catch him". People around me looked at me as though I was crazy and I kept running after the man who had taken my bag who was beginning to be a speck of dust among the crowds of shoppers. But I continued giving chase and screaming. Then my foot missed the pavement, my ankle twisted and I went down, hands first, my face and the rest of me. It was such a clumsy fall I feared I had lost my front teeth.

Under happier circumstances I would have laughed at myself whilst making sure that I rose quickly before many people saw me. That day I just lay there in a big heap wondering what was happening to me.

As one old man slowly came to my rescue and tried to lift me up, I realised I could not walk. My foot was aching terribly, sending electric spasms all over my body. I tried to stretch and twist my leg, it was torture. Tears came rolling down my cheeks. My ankle was beginning to swell. I sat there in pain and wished I could die.

Soon I realised there wasn't anything I could accomplish sitting there and feeling sorry for myself. I then held tightly on to the old man who was insisting that he should stretch my ankle and put it into its socket. I would not hear of that. Instead I hobbled, with a skirt full of dust and a face smudged with mascara, up to the shops. The first shop was a men's outfitters. When I entered, two salesmen came rushing and said they had no money for beggars. I almost went hysterical with laughter. Me, a beggar, that was all I wanted to hear. Anyway, I told them what had happened to me, and all I was asking of them was to phone the emergency bank number to try and stop payment on my account.

In no time, they started phoning. They must have phoned fourteen banks to find the secret number without any luck. Just then an idea flashed in my mind. What if the thug should get a brainwave of going for my car while I stood there. Without alerting anybody, I again hobbled out towards the car. The pain was unbearable and my ankle had swollen as though I suffered from elephantiasis. Each step was agony. I did not know what was best to do to ease the pain. Whether to keep moving or sit down. However I could not sit. I had to get to the car.

One of the saving graces about Hillbrow is that nobody takes notice of anyone out there. One could lie dying in any of those streets and nobody would care to know what is going on. So nobody seemed to take any notice of me as I struggled along.

I found the car just as I had left it and sat down. Leaning against it I told myself it was time I started thinking. With my bag gone with all my important belongings I had to think of how to get out of Hillbrow. It was already in the afternoon and soon night would fall. I had to act fast. I did not have a cent on me to telephone anybody.

Just then three young executive looking guys walked past me. One gave me a scrutinizing look and asked "Mama, are you alright?" I told him I was not and that I had been mugged and was sitting there stranded. They retraced their steps and came for more details. They seemed touched by my sad story and offered help. I gave them a few numbers to call and to tell whoever they found where to find the spare car keys.

It must have been over an hour when a friend came to my rescue. He was on the S.O.S list I had written out for the guys. Having told him what happened, he looked at my ankle and asked "Do you think you can drive with that foot?" I had not thought of that. I tried to stand up and could not. What were we to do? He could not drive two cars. The only option was for him to drive my car to some parking garage until Monday or the day when I could drive. We took the groceries out of my car and into his and we drove off.

As we were driving off, I kept thinking to myself, such bad luck can only happen to me. Why on earth couldn't those guys have raised anybody else but him? He wasn't actually my friend. The two of us suffered a love-hate relationship. In a way I was guilty of exploiting his availability and he was getting fed up with helping me and getting nothing in return for it.

It was as if he had been reading my mind. For suddenly he looked at me and said: "I must be the greatest fool you have ever met." With my eyes wide open I asked what he meant. "I mean you are not prepared to do me a favour, in fact, you think you are better class than me, but when you are in trouble, I am the first person you seek out. I am getting sick and tired of you." Did I hear someone say "you don't kick someone when he's down?" At first I told myself I was going to ignore him, but the more he recriminated me the more I felt sick of him. As we approached Baragwanath Hospital, I felt I had heard enough and I was not going to subject myself to more abuse.

"Stop the car, I want to get off," I said.

Without even asking why I wanted to alight and how did I hope to get home, he stopped the car. I lifted my aching foot, got out of his car and sat on the pavement. I watched him disappear into the townships.

Many cars drove past and none of them were people I knew. After a long time a car driven by youngsters stopped. I heard one of them telling the driver that they should ask if I needed help. Some yelled that I was a drunk. However one of the boys got out of the car and asked me what the trouble was. I told him and he looked at my foot which was quite huge and shiny. He called his friends to come and carry me into the car.

The car was obviously a stolen car. And they were not too sober. However I was past caring about what would happen if the police found us or the possibilities of driving into a pole. Frankly, I didn't think the driver had a licence. And I didn't even want to think what if these boys should get ideas of raping me. They carefully placed me in the back seat and made sure I was comfortable. I gave them directions to my house and closed my eyes trying to get some sleep. My whole body was shaking and shivering. One of the boys gave me a bottle of brandy and I took a huge bitter gulp, washed it down with coke and prayed for sleep.

I woke up as they drove into my street. I told them where to stop and they assisted me into my yard. My neighbour brought my house key and opened up while the boys carried me to my bed. Who said our youths were thugs, I thought as they were being tender with me. I thanked them profusely and asked them to call around for tea when next they were in the area.

Later in the evening my friend brought my groceries which had stayed in his car. I formally thanked him and watched him go. My neighbours had been around, massaging and giving me all the medication and help I needed.

Came Monday I was the first to enter the bank when the doors opened. I was offered a chair and as I was speaking to the teller, a man came to the little glass partitioned office. The teller looked up to tell him she was still attending to me; she will be with him shortly. Instead the man fixed his gaze on me and asked: "Is your name Mrs Mathiane?" I said it was.

Out of a bag he was carrying he fished my bag out. I opened my mouth and he interrupted me by saying: "I saw the guy grab it from you and I gave chase. I caught him next to the Hillbrow hospital and I beat him to a pulp. However, I must apologise that I had to take 50 cents from your purse to make a few phone calls trying to trace you." I thanked him and took my bag. I opened it to check if all my documents were intact. The twenty rand note as well as a few rands and cents fell out of my purse. For all I care, he need not have mentioned the 50 cents he had used as I would not have noticed if he had used as much as R5. My card was there and so was my cheque book. My passport, my accounts documents, the numerous cards as well as a few scraps of reading material. I was now more shocked at getting my bag back than I had been at losing it.

As I rummaged in my bag, I suddenly realised that I had not asked for my saviour's name and address. When I lifted my eyes from the bag, I was confronted by an empty wall.

He was gone.

16

The fire and the football club

A TEACHER from the school opposite the Mandela house tells of
how at about 10.30 on the morning of Thursday 28 July, he saw
a crowd of schoolboys running towards the Mandela house.

"As that no longer happens in Soweto, I wondered what was going
on. The State of Emergency long put an end to that. It was quite
common from 1984 to see a mob of students rushing off to fight or set
a house on fire. But now in '88 that is a strange sight.

"So when I saw a sea of boys coming down the street, first I thought
they could be coming to our school. Perhaps they wanted our students
to join them on some activity. Some of the teachers had already seen
what was going on and had joined me outside. We saw them go past
and we heaved a sigh of relief. We then thought they could be going
to the next school. No, instead they went straight up to the Mandela
home.

"We held our breaths. We knew there was going to be some form of
confrontation. They surrounded the house and called out names.
Nobody responded. Soon they climbed the walls. In no time, we heard
glass break and doors being kicked.

"There was commotion in the yard and I prayed and hoped that
there should be nobody in the house. I wondered where the helper and
Mandela's grandchildren were. I thought of the vicious dog. I
wondered what would happen should the football club make an
appearance.

"Then we saw smoke, followed by flames. I could not believe it.
Mandela's house was burning. My colleagues came out, as well as

the students. The township street was soon full of people. People came running from other streets, or out of cars and taxis.

"They seemed to be immobilised and watch as if in a trance. The women who are great for screaming or ordering that something be done stood like zombies, watching without betraying any emotion. And so were the men. It is not as if the students were stopping anybody from doing anything. They just stood by.

"We listened to the sound of electrical gadgets explode. High into the sky the smoke went and more people came. Soon the police came to join us, followed by the ambulance. But they did nothing. Not even ask questions. They just watched as the flames leapt.

"Then came the blackjacks [the Soweto City Council police]. They are great for instilling fear in people. For one, they hang on the van double doors and alight while the vehicle is in motion. This is done to scare whoever is in trouble. Anyway they arrived in that spectacular fashion and then did nothing but parade the area dragging their heavy boots while their rifles hung on their shoulders. If the South African Police could simply stand and watch, who are the blackjacks to take action?

"The last to come was the fire brigade. They arrived with all the agility and pomp of professionals. They got off the truck and rushed around fixing their paraphernalia. But alas! They had no water in their tanks. They mounted their vehicle again, with the same dexterity and flair. Orlando West has been suffering many water cuts as the government tries to shatter what is left of the rent boycott. In fact lately they have been turning on water briefly at midnight, so we have had midnight alarms sounding as people wake each other to fill containers while they can.

"Anyway I suppose that did not help the firemen. I could not help to think of the olden days when Soweto was without a fire-station and houses were razed to the ground before a fire brigade could be summoned from town. Days when people would die because there was no telephone around to summon an ambulance from town.

"We helplessly waited while the billows of smoke went up and it was becoming obvious that nothing could be salvaged from the house. In fact we were fearing that the next houses would soon catch fire.

"Then the brigade arrived again and in no time were doing what we always marvelled at as little boys, that is men fighting fire.

"At about that time, we saw her silver Mercedes Benz arrive.

"I have been an ardent admirer of this woman. I am always stunned by her beauty and her strength. As my school is quite near the house, I have caught a glimpse of her arrogance and action a few times, such as when telling someone to get off or chastising some of the boys staying in her house. Frankly I have never wished to cross paths with her.

"She drove slowly up the road and parked the car. At that point all eyes shifted from the inferno to her. From nowhere, her boys appeared and so did reporters. She did not say a word. There was neither tear nor smile. Her face displayed no emotion as she looked at what up to that morning was her house. She coldly looked at the reporters who were throwing questions at her. At that stage I hated the reporters for hounding her. I did not understand how those heartless people could have the temerity to want an interview at a time when she was watching her house, her life, her possessions go up in flames. I have seen her many faces but the one I saw that morning was a heart-rending spectacle. There was silence as she made her U-turn and drove off with reporters fast on her tail.

"The fire subsided — although not before the fire brigade had run out of water a second time. Police began to activate themselves. The firemen started clearing the rubble. Slowly people drifted away, hushed.

"One thing that surprises me was that later the Mandela family advisers made statements thanking the people for cleaning up. The firemen cleaned up, the crowd did nothing, everyone just stood and watched."

Westcliff in Orlando West is one of the oldest townships in Soweto. It still boasts of old citizens and founders of Soweto. People there not only know each other but they know everybody's parents as well as grandparents.

If you are looking for a family around this township, you will be told the house will be next to so-and-so's house who did or does such-and-such. The township has its heroes and its thugs. But more than that, the township has always been in the news. After all it is a proud home for a number of political families. There is the Mandela family, the Sisulus, the Mathews and the Mothopengs. Also around there is Tutu's house and Lucy Mvubelo's house. Perched on the little hillock is Orlando West High where incidentally the first victim of the student uprisings of 1976, Hector Petersen, was shot dead.

Before the advent of black consciousness, people referred to those living in this area as *abelungu abamnyama*, meaning whites who are black. This area was initially earmarked for middle-class blacks, three bedrooms and bathrooms. The brickwork is different from the rest of the townships. Even the lay-out is different. Here the streets are broad and the main streets have always been tarred. There are oak trees lining the streets. It was meant to be a model township.

The township does not have a history of political involvement besides the few meetings which the late James Sofasonke Mpanza used to hold, but the people have always been in the know of what is happening. They witnessed a number of their neighbours lose husbands by way of imprisonment and deaths. They became familiar with slogans, political unrests and changes — more than people of other townships.

So when the Mandela Football Club came into being, people openly spoke about it. At first they were quite intrigued.

"When Winnie went to Brandfort, we read she had started a creche and had some community projects" said a woman living in Westcliff. "So when I heard of the football club, I though she was starting a youth club. Remember, those were the days when children were boycotting schools. I really thought she was onto something good but as you know, it was far from that." She then went on to describe the boys as a terror to the neighbourhood.

People around the area do not want to have anything to say about what has happened. However they share one thing in common — they regret that the house belongs to Mandela and not to Winnie. According to them, they wished there was a way the students could have dealt with the football club without touching Mandela's house.

While the name of Mandela remains a symbol of government resistance and inspires hope into people's hearts, the football club has been another matter. It spelt death and destruction to many.

"It is not as if we do not know who these boys are. They have grown up right under our noses. We know their parents and we know how their parents feel about what their children are doing," said one woman.

That is a strange thing. In the other townships people do not know the comrades. During '86 in particular, the boys you would see rampaging down the streets were not boys from your own township. They were from somewhere else. Maybe your boys were rampaging there. But in Orlando West it is different. The boys of the football club throw their weight around at the very same people who had changed their nappies and wiped their noses.

"Ma-so-and-so whose son is part of the club is such a bitter woman. She was telling us how she had donated her son to Winnie. She cried saying while Winnie had lost a husband she wants us to lose our sons."

Another said: "One of the boys was being chased by the police for stealing a car. He dumped it right in front of my house. Do you know what the cops do when they chase car thieves? They shoot and do not care who is hit by a bullet. You can then imagine how I felt when I saw the boy get into my yard and jump the fence with the cops behind him. And woe unto you if the police should find your innocent 16 year old boy in the house. Your child will be bundled up and be taken to the police station."

Another woman interjected by saying, "I have had boys run into my house and sit in all innocence, pretending to be my sons doing their homework. The police come and question, and if you deny that he is your child, you are a dead duck. You stand there and lie while inwardly you wish they could lock him up and throw the key away."

While the debate rages on as to why Mandela's house was gutted, people feel it had been coming a long time. Although most regret that it is Mandela's house that has been destroyed, people living around the area have a lot to tell.

"What happened to the old lady whose house was destroyed by comrades only for them to admit they put the wrong house on fire? The struggle does seem to be self-serving. Which of the leaders ever compensated the poor woman? In the end it was poor Father Nkwe from the White City Jabavu who offered her some help."

"Let her also feel what less powerful people felt when their homes were destroyed. She is the one after all who spoke of the matches — he who rides the tiger ends up in its belly," said one of the women.

After the fire came the arrest of 22 boys from the Daliwonga High School. One of the students said the police got to the school one morning and collected a number of boys. When they came back hours later, all the boys were assembled. The police then instructed the boys they had been questioning to point out the culprits. When the police were told they did not know who was responsible, the police then picked on 22 boys.

One boy described standing in formation while the police walked through the lines, picking here and there apparently at random.

People whose sons attend the Daliwonga High School are living in fear. Since the Mandela fire, two families have been attacked and their houses set on fire. For some time the sight of AK 47 rifles has been common in the area, mainly at night-time. Now they are to be seen in broad daylight too.

17

Of good neighbourliness and abundant parenthood

———————— AUGUST/SEPTEMBER 1988 ————————

SO much is said about black culture by people who least understand it. While African culture may not be the best in the world, it does hold society together. For instance, in practice there were no orphans. Nor was there adoption or any need for adoption. If, as a woman, your sister should die, her children automatically become yours. That is why we do not have titles such as "aunt". You were either referred to as "small mother" or become "elder mother" depending of course where in the hierarchy of siblings you fell.

The same went for men. Any of your brothers' children would be yours. And they would address their uncles, "small" or "elder" father. That is why there are jokes about whites asking a black person as to how many times have they buried their mother.

That relationship made provision for natural adoption in the event of one of the parents dying.

An elder in the family is treated with the greatest respect and officiates at funerals and weddings. At funerals he is the one who washes the corpse and makes sure the family rituals are properly done. At weddings he will be consulted on the rituals and proceedings as well as accepting gifts on behalf of the important members of the family. They do not only stand in for those who have since departed, they are also the link between the living and the dead. For instance in the case of a young man dying and leaving behind a young bride, one of the brothers becomes husband to that woman. Preferably, one who is single. The idea is not only to keep the woman in the family, but a means to secure the dead man's family as well as perpetuate his name. The children born out of that union are not his. They are regarded as those of his dead brother.

This means whoever as taken over his brother's wife still has to get his own wife who will bear him children. The two sets of kids will grow up as brothers and sisters, and who says they are not?

This brings me to bigamy. Present-day society frowns at a man who has two wives and yet accepts as the norm one who has a mistress. Those who question the latter man are accused of being old-fashioned, out of tune with contemporary morality. It is not important that his children are abusive to the mistress at the slightest opportunity and he has his wife screaming at him day in and day out. Society will fondly refer to him as "isoka" (ladies man). In other cultures they use others words, but admire him all the same.

This man will most likely be irresponsible. Most of the time his wife will be running the house while he squanders his money and affection outside the home.

If he introduces the idea of legalising his lover's status, his wife may at first hit the roof. But when she realises that her husband means to go ahead with the idea, she learns to live with it. The situation might be that there is mutual respect as each woman knows where her place is. For instance there is no way that either woman could be abusive to the other if they met in the street. What is likely to happen is that they will at all times present a pleasant countenance in order to gain respect from the husband. Their children will look up to these women as "mothers" and as they are not likely to be living under the same roof, chances of conflicts are minimised. Children born in such a setting take each other as brother and sister. They do not have to play the hide and seek game which is the case with the children of the man who has a permanent mistress.

The children of a mistress may be on cordial terms with their mother's lover but they soon learn not to accost him in public. His wife might know who they are and be abusive towards them. In fact in most cases, the children are resentful to him. Meanwhile there is no peace in his own home. The wife will know the husband is messing around. She might even know the name of the woman. They will be screaming at each other and eventually the children get to know about it and start despising their father. It is only when they grow older and understand the ways of the world that they empathise with both parents. But in most cases that is when a lot of damage has been done.

Life is certainly different with the polygamous one. His wife knows exactly what is happening. If she needs to raise him for an urgent matter she knows where to find him. Everything is done above board.

She knows he is not cavorting all over the show. It is common among black women that when an unmarried woman is questioned about messing around with a married man, her reply is "where am I to get mine from because if I should resort to a dog the other bitches will bite me to death."

Polygamy was also a means by which people shared wealth. It was common practice for poor men to marry their daughters off to rich men such as chiefs. Chief Matubatuba in the 19th century lived to the age of 90 years. Even at that age, young maidens were being brought to him as brides. Nobody was being fooled that he played a meaningful role as a husband or father. His Indunas probably kept his home fires burning. But the girls' parents were happy, the girls had an opportunity to carve a niche for themselves, and he was happy. I am told that he would stroke the young maidens' cheeks and say "I'll deal with you one day" and thereby retire into his hut.

So when one reads stories of how children are abused by their parents in some so-called civilised parts of the world then one is inclined to think perhaps Africans had a superior culture after all. For instance, there is no way that a child can die out of hunger like the one who died recently in London. The parents are alleged to have fed their dog and moved off to the pub leaving the child screaming with hunger. The post mortem revealed that parts of the baby's napkin were found in the infant's intestines. The neighbours were not even aware that there was a child. And I am told it is quite normal for such behaviour in that society. They call it mind your own business.

That would not have happened in our society because no man is an island there. There is no way a couple could live all by themselves without the neighbours wondering what they are up to. We have unpaid social workers who although we accuse them of being gossip mongers, however, like it or not, serve a need. Although we do not like it when they poke their noses in people's business, they act as ombudsmen.

Besides, there are certain things that are not done. Although we may sometimes have embraced foreign standards, there are still traditions that we cling to. Such as going to offer condolences when a member of your street has had a misfortune. Helping with baking when there is a wedding in your street, or that men help with the slaughtering. Elder women still rally around a woman who has given birth. They will bring porridge for her to eat to get fat and strong, some will offer to wash the nappies. The infant will be their concern for a period of about three years. They will inquire after its health and watch its progress.

Speaking to an elderly white friend whose house has suddenly become too big with the husband dead and children away, she told me she was selling and moving to a flat. It seemed rather a shame to move from her old residence where even though her neighbours might not have cared to know anything about her, at least their servants, being friendly to hers, were part of her life. They used to come to her house at the time her husband died. They used to walk right into her bedroom and force her to have a bath and eat. She often told me that without their concern she would have died.

I call my neighbours unpaid security guards. Nobody can freely walk into my yard and do as he pleases. If the children are away on holiday and I am all by myself, I never feel I am alone. If for instance they have not seen me around noon, they will come or send a child to investigate as to what I am up to. I do not regard that as being nosy. The fact is I am a woman with children and they are men and bother themselves to know that I am fine. And in the event of anything happening, they know my people will inquire first from them as to what happened.

There is a popular phrase among neighbours which goes something like: "you are the one who will close my eyes before my people come," at least the immediate mess will have been cleaned and cleared by the neighbours. They are very important people in one's life.

18

The swing of the pendulum

ORLANDO Main Road is one of the oldest roads in Soweto. It separates and links innumerable townships, and it also separates people. Next to Uncle Tom's Hall, on the right at a corner stands a small cottage with flowers. That is Zephania Mothopheng's house. Crossing the road on the left is a house secured in a concrete wall with a lawn. That is Nelson Mandela's house, now rebuilt from the fire.

The two have much in common. Both are long-term prisoners. Both are presidents of banned organisations, Mothopeng the Pan-Africanist Congress and Mandela the African National Congress. Both were once comrades in the same organisation, the ANC Youth League, which disbanded when the Pan-Africanist Congress came into being.

For many years the ANC was the only liberation movement in South Africa. But then after World War II disenchanted young members grew tired of "knocking on the door" and formed the more militant Youth League. Then came the drawing up of the Freedom Charter in 1955. The Africanists rejected it and in April 1959 the Pan-Africanist Congress was born at the Donaldson Hall in Orlando.

In no time the PAC made itself felt. It called for the people to refuse to carry passes. Despite the opposition of the ANC, the call was widely heeded. The country was plunged into chaos. Except for the Bambatha Rebellion at the turn of the century, the South African regime had never been so powerfully challenged. On 21 March 1960 the Sharpeville massacre took place. The pass protest had turned tragic. Yet the infant PAC had equalled the venerable ANC in stature, with the Paarl uprising and the march on Cape Town causing more stir than anything the ANC had done in fifty years.

The government soon squashed both organisations. They went into exile, at war not only with the regime but with each other.

To this day the PAC claims it started the revolution, and that it had trained cadres, in places like Egypt, long before the ANC. But it has had nothing to show of its existence except wrangles and tragedies.

Some blamed power-struggles among the leaders. Others put the blame on the absence of liberals (meaning whites), leading to financial constraints. For whatever reasons, the PAC seemed to have died while the ANC rode the crest. In 1986 while "Release Mandela" calls ran high, the PAC central committee met in Dar-es-Salaam and elected another prisoner of Pretoria, Zephania Mothopheng, as president.

If the idea was to provide an alternative symbol to Mandela, it did not work as far as the media are concerned. The PAC remains deep in the shadows. It is seen by nearly all respectable commentators as merely a joke organisation, doing even less than the ANC to actually bring about the liberation everybody talks about.

Despite this there are many PAC people in South Africa. It is today more easy than for years to hear them speaking openly, and they seem very little worried by the common treatment of the ANC as a government in waiting. They are confident that come open elections they will win hands down. They draw a parallel with the Zimbabwe struggle, pointing out that for years Nkomo was seen as the father of Zimbabwe nationalism while Mugabe was ignored by the liberal press. When the time came, Nkomo was nowhere.

They say they are discriminated against by the Western press because the West wants to see a "compromise faction" (ie the ANC) inherit South Africa and not a true "nationalist movement" (the PAC).

It has become quite common at gatherings to see the singing of the African Anthem accompanied either by the clenched fist or with the open-hand salute of the Pan-Africanists. For many years past it was either sung with the clenched fist or hands down. (Strangely, the ANC's raised thumb has been overtaken by the clenched fist, which started as a Black Consciousness salute.)

At the same time it is no longer strange to hear people greeting with the Africanist slogan "Izwe Lethu" (Our Land). At a "neutral" party recently I was surprised to hear guests entering with "Izwe Lethu" as if that was entirely conventional. At funerals you can see the open-hand salute openly.

The fact that today even students at the Soweto College of Education are openly identifying with the Africanists is also a pointer. For the past several years, there was no way a symposium with speakers

such as Sipho Sepamla, Paul Maake and Prof Njabulo Ndebele —
Africanist protagonists — could have taken place at that campus. That
used to be UDF territory. But now that symposium has been held.

If one is to go by the graffiti in the townships and read anything into
that, then one can say there are less and less signs of UDF and ANC
lately. Although that does not necessarily mean they have been replaced by those of the PAC.

Azapo has been assumed to be an offspring of the PAC. It is often
considered an "internal wing" in the same way the UDF is called an "internal wing" of the ANC.

Questioning Azapo on this marriage one gets the feeling that there
is no love lost between the two. Some Azapo members say the PAC
are confused in wanting to include whites in their Africanism.

"PAC says anyone who owes allegiance to Africa is an African. That
means any white who calls himself an African is an African," complains
one Azapo member.

Azapo accepts anybody who is discriminated against by white rule.
This includes Indians and coloureds, regardless of how privileged they
may be. Some people feel Azapo is unfair in including Indians and
coloureds as they come from different backgrounds to those of black
people.

For instance when applying for overseas scholarships, the Indians
get the bulk of the money because they are studying Masters and
fancy degrees while the black-black is battling on a first degree maybe.
They also enter politics as academics and experts to lead the less educated masses, who are the blacks. Another thought describes Indians
as the merchant class with blacks being the workers.

This is a déjà vu of the feelings which resulted in the creation of
SASO. Then the feeling was to put whites on one side and Indians and
blacks and coloureds together on the other. Now there is talk that Indians and coloureds belong on the other side.

To Azapo, the PAC was a phase in history which is now outmoded.
That is exactly the same as the ANC says about Azapo and Black
Consciousness. Yet the PAC casts itself as the modern one, and the
other two as outdated phases. The PAC people say it is they who
recognise only one race, the human race. Their big objection is that the
ANC and the Freedom Charter recognise "national groups".

Recently at a union seminar, Cunningham Ngcukana of Nactu
spoke of "African workers" while Phandelani Nefholovodvhe, also of
Nactu, referred to "black workers". Most of their union members
don't bother about such polemics; to them both words mean the
same. Yet many eyebrows were raised at the seminar. People saw a
split coming up between Africanist and BC, and indeed at the congress

the Africanists moved in strongly. Now the BC people, who have been their fellow-travellers for many years, feel themselves kicked in the teeth.

One swallow does not make a summer, but the Nactu incident is just one of many indications of a new era. BC and Africanists have needed each other to survive at all against the non-racial Cosatu giant. Now it is obvious that theirs was a marriage of convenience. It is still convenient, but the question is whether the convenience is strong enough to outweigh the hostilities, or will the 30-year-long two-part tradition of black politics turn into a full-scale three-way split?

While Africanism is on the rise internally, the poor reputation of the PAC in exile is unchanged. The mediocre leadership is legendary. The organisation has been bogged down with problems ranging from fatal power-struggles to drug-peddling charges. Moreover, the PAC's literature seems to be very antiquated. To this day it still distributes materials which refer to ancient notions such as the "United States of Africa" and language like "dialectical struggle" which seems to be borrowed from olden-days Russia. Like the ANC in exile, the PAC seems oblivious to the changing situations of black people at home. Whatever upsurge in Africanism there has been, it is unlikely that it is thanks to input from abroad.

One school of thought maintains that the rise of Africanism is simply because of the decline of the UDF. They credit that partly to the reign of terror which was experienced in the townships, which was identified with the UDF. Partly also it may be because the Charterists have been the dominant faction for some time. They have long been promising that "victory is ours", but the people see no victory and lose faith.

Meanwhile the PAC has also been offering unfulfilled promises. There is not much difference between its promises and the ANC's promises, but the ANC's have been heard and the PAC's have not been heard, which is the PAC's good luck.

At the same time there has always been a "gut feeling" for Africanism rumbling in many people's souls. As one person says there is no way one could wish Africanism away in Africa. "We are in Africa. All these non-racialist and power-sharing strategies are time-buying gimmicks. It would be a different matter if we were Africans in America, we would be begging for a place in the sun, but this is South Africa and we are the rightful heirs. If you look closely at the ANC, you will notice that even they are becoming Africanist. Of course we understand that they are bound by the presence of whites not to come out as honestly as they would like to, but down the ladder you have the 1976 lot and the '80 lot. Those speak the Africanist language through and through."

Meanwhile on the BC front, with the rug pulled from their feet they stand exposed for their lack of adult support. They rally students and young intellectuals, who "graduate out" as they get older.

Maybe as we saw the rise and fall of the UDF we are witnessing the crescent of the PAC, time will tell.

From the point of view of the black person in the townships, none of the political movements are achieving. The differences between them are sometimes what only high-grade intellectuals can understand. For instance most Africanists are no more "anti" the ordinary individual white man than the Charterists are. They are only anti the idea that the whites should have a separate position in South Africa, and in fact the Charterists are also anti this idea, whatever their acknowledgement of "national groups" actually means.

It comes down to the fact that everybody is fed up with white rule but nobody knows how to end it, so everybody turns on each other and nobody makes progess.

19

Pointed fingers

FOR years, there has been the phenomenon of finger-pointing among the black organisations. Until recently the pointing has been about who is more "relevant" with each group claiming that no-one but itself does any good. The finger-pointing is most fierce at dinners or occasions to welcome representatives of foreign funding agencies. During the open part of the proceedings everyone is very polite, butter not melting in their mouths. But as soon as one project has the ear of the guest of honour in private, there will be all sorts of tales about the faults of all the others.

Now another aspect is rearing its head, whereby various rivals are accusing each other of being CIA agents. This comes from the fact that many organisations are on the USAID dole. Educational, business, and social welfare projects receive money from USAID, but it has become a habit for recipients to pretend they are not receiving any money from this fund. They carry on as if they were completely removed, and label those who openly admit to receiving USAID as agents of the CIA.

A recent example is of a women's project which received a USAID grant to get it off the ground. Later the women approached a prominent local trust which administers foreign funding, and they were told they did not qualify for funds, as they had received a sum from USAID. The "official" reason for turning them down was that USAID was already looking after them. Additionally, it was insinuated that they could not be trusted because USAID linked them to the CIA.

These reasons are preposterous. Who is not double funded? Or triple funded for that matter? We regularly see directors flying in and out of the country with their begging bowls, looking for added funds. We know that one donor is never enough, and that even the projects which have been taken under the wing of some or other corporation still look for further funds elsewhere.

The truth of the matter is that the trust turned down those women because their group does not toe a particular political line. Individually they have their own political affiliations, but not as an organisation. And there lies the problem.

When the various trusts were created, the aim was to assist under-privileged blacks. No particular ideology was supposed to be a criterion for assistance. But alas, gradually we saw a shift into rigid political positions. These days the criterion for assistance is that one's political stand is in accordance with those who are in trust of the funds.

The funding channels become politically coloured. Some have a BC/Africanist flavour. Inkatha has some sources of its own, and of course the majority are in the ANC/UDF/"progressive" camp. The trouble is that an organisation or project which does not wish to align itself with any particular camp will have a hard time.

Unfortunately this is spilling into the workplace as well. There are now institutions which ask prospective employees about their ideological leanings. The reason they give is to group like poles together. But we know there is more to grouping than meets the eye, and again the chief victim is the person who wants to do a job without being tied to any movement. The lesser victim is the person who wants to identify with a movement other than the "progressive" tendency, meaning the ANC/UDF fold, because the openings are few.

When the trusts go out lobbying for funds, they use every possible line of persuasion. They solicit the support of blacks from any political orientation to support their claims. But when they get the money, they distribute it only among people of their following.

Another disturbing factor is the using of funds. In one case an organisation was founded with good intentions, by dedicated people. The executives in the organisation then realised that they qualified for funding. They arranged a board to facilitate applying for funds.

Irregularities have come to the board's notice. The board started questioning the huge salary increases and the use of the organisation's funds for travel overseas. The executives replied by saying that it was not the board's business. The board said that the money belonged to the masses in whose name it had been donated. The executives wanted to know where were the masses when they started the organisation and put sweat and toil into getting it going.

Frankly speaking, most people do not care who gets money and what the recipients do with it, so long as they do not use the name of the suffering blacks to get rich. People should desist from collecting money claiming to be using it for poor blacks but instead giving it to privileged blacks. People don't mind those who go shooting their mouths off on sensitive issues so long as they do not claim to be speaking on behalf of the masses, especially when they never even address the constituencies they purport to be speaking for.

It would also be helpful if there was less finger-pointing at alleged informers. Whereas there surely are informers in many organisations, there is a dangerous habit of venting personal grudges by spreading word that so-and-so is unreliable.

This has recently happened to a person who is active in one of the so-called progressive organisations. For some time she drifted along, doing what everyone was doing. That is: worshipping the holy cows, not questioning statements, ostracising those who were being accused of disloyalty to the cause. Then suddenly people started drifting away from her, and she discovered that she was being called an informer. Her first thought was to resign, but on second thoughts she realised that would not solve the problem, it would instead confirm the rumour. She bravely assembled her comrades and confronted them.

At first they denied, but when she persisted they told her that word had come from Lusaka that she was working for the System. She then demanded an air ticket to go to Lusaka and clear it up. She got to Lusaka and of course nobody had anything to say against her. Now she is back and "in the clear" although there is always some mud that sticks. She believes that the whole business started from jealousy of her beauty, and she is now angry that such inflammatory stories can gain ground.

The sad thing is that she is not aware that she herself has been a holy cow. Had the organisation not turned on her, when would she have started doing her spring cleaning?

At the same time this woman complains strongly about the tendency for whites to run the affairs of the progressive organisations. She refers to the workshops which are always being conducted in town for the benefit of blacks. Her gripe is that black people should be taught how to run these workshops, and then run them on their own in the townships.

This issue has long been simmering, and it is now time it was openly brought out and discussed. On the one hand, those who complain have a case. The blacks often do not get a chance, faced with whites who in many cases are from the richest and most well-educated sector, confident and sometimes pushy. Some whites, also coloureds and Indians, get kicks from black dependence.

On the other hand one can ask why the complainers do not just go and do their thing. There are a number of whites who would love to give projects over to blacks and rest assured that they will continue. But unfortunately that has often not been the case. Some organisations have made a big noise about the blacks taking over, only to collapse a few months later. It is common also to see frail old ladies from the suburbs break their backs getting work done and some of the black leaders turn up in time to make speeches.

The other form of finger-pointing is at the funders who are alleged to discriminate against black-run organisations. In this case one can only recommend that the people who make this argument should look at the records of each organisation, to see what there is to show and how the money has been spent.

20

Hard to tell the wheat from the chaff

TEN years ago, a group of black children loitering in town during the day would not only have raised eyebrows, they would have been courting arrest. Remember, in those days rumour was rife about planned marches on the city. In fact some marches came nearly to fruition, before aborting.

However, when education came to a standstill in Soweto, schools mushroomed in areas such as Braamfontein, Fordsburg, and the city centre.

These schools are quasi-private, often with catchy names designed to make them relevant to the political climate.

Some operate through DET while others have gone beyond education as taught through DET. They have begun to introduce black students to do projects all by themselves (such things are not done in township schools) and they inculcate a sense of individualism and confidence. But they fall short of realising their dreams, because of financial constraints. Some are also trying to prepare students to cope with the more demanding standards of the Joint Matriculation Board or the British A and O level systems.

Then there is the other group of schools who are all out to make a quick buck. They are exploiting the parents and harming the children. One school has opened boarding facilities without having residential premises. Children unroll mattresses in the classrooms at night.

At first many parents saw these schools as an escape from the disruptions in township schools, but now complaints are common with parents saying they have gone out of the frying pan into the fire.

Many schools do not have enough teachers which means children idle most of the day. These are the children who are seen having lunch from as early as 11.00 am and afternoons they go to the movies.

Some of the schools have kept moving from place to place. Last year one moved three times, from downtown Johannesburg to Braamfontein and back to central city.

One in Randburg called itself a Christian school. There children learnt at "their own pace" said the Christian principal gentleman. The school has since moved to another white suburb and some children had to fall off for lack of means of transport. A transfer from that school proved difficult. Not only have places in township schools been taken up, but the reports from that school were hardly comprehensible. Nor did the name of the school appear on the report. Children who had sought refuge at the Randburg school saw themselves back where they had been two years ago.

Principals say it is hard to find premises except in places where landlords are desperate for tenants. "I called a meeting with my students to tell them we are here on sufferance. I told them to avoid using the lift, not to talk outside the classrooms and never to write on the walls," said one. In '86 and '87, the chief feature of Witwatersrand schooling was the exodus from the townships to town. It now seems that the beginning of 1989 will see a reverse exodus, back to the townships, which now seem to offer the best hope of normal schooling. Furthermore, schooling is far cheaper in Soweto than in town. Most of the schools in town charge around R100 per month for school fees. On top of that students supply their own stationery and books. Whereas the DET supplies schools with stationery, and school fees are no longer paid (although there is a school levy determined by the principal and his board.)

At some of the town schools, children even now near year end do not have prescribed books. "You find students eating expensive meals which even teachers cannot afford but they will tell you they have no money for the books. I sometimes wonder if their parents know what their children are up to," said a teacher at one of the Braamfontein schools.

People who work in town frequently remark about the meals these children afford to eat. They patronise fast foods joints while their counterparts at private school either carry lunch packs from home or buy from subsidised canteens, and the township children usually have lunches of fatcake and chips.

There is a common opinion that the parents of the town-school children often have no clue what their children are doing. "How many bother to look at the children's books? How do they afford to give the child R40 a week for pocket money? If people are being exploited it is because they allow it to happen," says one educationist.

One problem is the weak educational background, aggravated by several years of unstable learning and politicking. "We have to unteach so many things," says a teacher.

The other problem is money. One school in Braamfontein has seven classrooms, 180 students and 21 teachers — 7 full time and 14 part-time. The rent is R5 000 per month. Even with the relatively high fees, the school depends heavily on sponsorship from companies and organisations. At the schools which are initiated and run by blacks, it is often said that the money goes more easily to white-manned schools. But some teachers deny this and point to white-run schools which have as much or more difficulty raising funds. The uncertainty makes it difficult to attract teachers. One teacher says: "People want security, they want to know that their careers are not only meaningful but that they are secure. Commitment alone is not enough. Such schools do not have housing loans and subsidies. They could be there today and gone tomorrow."

A long-serving Soweto principal says that some of the town schools have employed teachers who would never be taken on at DET schools. "There is overcrowding and no direction. One wonders if those children were not better off in a DET classroom."

Presently it is difficult to know which school is doing good work because education has been unstable. Even the end of year results cannot be effectively used to judge the performance of the school. There are a number of factors that go towards a school becoming a place for learning. Apart from the three R's, discipline and social responsibility must be taken into account.

21

Jam in the bubblegum

BLACK music has come under heavy attack lately, with critics freely handing out terms varying from "bubblegum" to "trash". However, some of the most widely-criticised musicians are singing their way to the bank.

It has been said that a country gets the leaders it deserves. That is true about the state of black arts today, where cultural insolvency is following in the wake of political despair. The "respectable" writers are offering no challenges. Like a record with a scratch, they keep roving and raving about the same old point — black suffering. No wonder then that the "respectable" writers are fading into the background. They are praised and discussed in the media, while the songs that top the charts consist of meaningless escapism. Of local songs which are currently in the big time, the themes are such things as ghosts, pineapple jam, taxis, and a pair of small takkies.

In a country endowed with a beautiful landscape and with interesting people whose lifestyles are more diverse than anywhere else in the world, there is no song that is about South Africa, nor about any of the interesting towns and peoples.

There are songs about L.A., Last Train to Georgia, April in Paris, foggy London, Chicago, New York, even Amsterdam. But there is nothing about Johannesburg or Hillbrow or Durban. An attempt was made on Soweto by Clarence Carter — a visiting American musician — but that has not been able to stand the test of time.

There are those who maintain that life is unbearable and does not lend much to creativity. They say that like the children of Israel who cried by the rivers of Babylon, blacks must hang their harps and wallow in oppression. But even the children of Israel made music in Babylon, and in any case the bulk of blacks do not spend all day every day in misery, and do not appreciate their singers and songwriters telling them to do so.

On a recent trip abroad I was struck by comments of people who had never been to South Africa. They thought that all of life here consisted of fear and fighting. They found it impossible to visualise that come Friday night the townships contain masses of fun-lovers scuttling this way and that in search of liveliness. On Saturday mornings pedestrians and motorists give way to bridal parties in cars lined with ribbons with hooters at full blast. Drive around the streets and tell me if you do not see lovers walking and laughing. Families still get together in observance of rituals ranging from paying lobola to unveiling tombstones. Christening parties and 21st birthdays are common. Stokvels of various kinds are in order over weekends. And yet this kind of activity is ignored by the writers and artists who claim to be relevant.

Some people blame the cultural boycott for the low standard. "It is thanks to politicians like Azapo and the UDF that today we are exposed to this rubbish that is called music," said one critic. Others defend the boycott but claim it has had the wrong effect: "The boycott has not made us turn into ourselves and be more creative, instead we have trash blaring on our radios all the time."

One view is that as long as foreign artists perform in South Africa, local artists will always be rated second however good they may be. Muntu Myeza says that were it not for the boycott we would not have had the Brenda Fassies and the Yvonne Chaka-Chakas. "Our artists always served as supporting numbers, while American has-beens and unknowns were treated like royalty."

Sipho Sepamla, director of the Federated Union of Black Arts, said he is not bothered about the standards or lack of standards. "These are experimental years. Artists are experimenting with sound. Music is a reflection of the times and in South Africa there is a great deal of growing going on. We are discovering ourselves and are coming to grips with our continent and our corner. We are seeing the birth of a South African sound."

Victor Ntoni, a renowned bassist, is one of many people unhappy about where music is going. "Society applauds any silly thing which is marketed well enough; the media don't know what they are writing about; and illiteracy amongst musicians is appalling", he says. He maintains that much of the problem lies with the black music critics. "They write PR pieces — 'the show was superb', or 'she wowed her fans'. That sort of writing does not give us a constructive appreciation. I have been in countries where journalists on the music beats were musicians themselves. Come evening the reporter would produce his trumpet and join his group.

"Such a person knows what he is dealing with. I am not saying that every reporter must be an instrumentalist, but that they should acquaint themselves with what it takes to deliver constructive comment. They cannot simply hand out meaningless praise all the time to be popular with the artists."

Ntoni says that young artists have become complacent. They cannot read and write music, and do not want to learn. They are unable to rise to challenges, but are content if they sell on a basis of sheer luck and absence of competition.

While it is commonplace to allege that the artists, especially black artists, are ripped off by the studios, not everyone blames it all on the studios. A veteran musician, who has backed many big names for twenty years, maintains that it has become the custom to do anything to appear on TV and get applause. "Some stars are only looking at the purse and could not be bothered if the song is good or bad. They sign contracts which they do not understand and don't even bother to get copies for themselves. They get a big sum in advance and think it is Christmas. Thereafter the bulk of the money goes to the producers and managers. The artists take peanuts home. Some producers, black or white, steal people's music and call it theirs. If musicians used their heads, they would have their songs copyrighted before entering the studios. Musicians need an organisation to protect them against exploitation. But there is too much bickering to get it right."

Meanwhile the old guard who used to fill township halls, singing of township life, has disappeared. Their songs were about migrant life, lovers coming to the city, the train from Pimville collecting people all the way to town, and such things. Those were well thought out songs, with ballads such as "Lakutsoni 'langa" being regarded as evergreens and still widely sung in homes and private gathering-places. In most cases the composers and artists died poor.

Kippie Moeketsi is a classic example. He played township sounds with a jazz orientation, and died a pauper. Now he is commemorated with a smart club in the Market complex.

This is a thing he would never have believed possible, but it does not do him any good.

The survivors of the township music pioneers — such as Thoko Mgcina, Dolly Rathebe and Thandi Klaassen — are an endangered species. They and their contemporaries, now dead or exiled, popularised western music emulating people like Ella Fitzgerald and Lena

Horne. But they also took great pride in their own music. Among Thoko's hits is "Mangwane", about a delinquent young man pleading with his aunt. This number cuts right across generation and colour, and Thoko's forté has been to reach both young and old. She has the ability to take an ordinary children's ditty such as "Meadowlands", a song of resistance to the Sophiatown removals, and sing it in such a way that it bears meaning. At the same time she can handle gospel either in the way the Black Americans do it or in the passionate fashion of the Zion Christians who go into spiritual frenzies in all corners of South Africa each Sunday. And she does all that without being sexual. She simply spreads her arms and sings.

Nobody hears much about these artists. Dolly was regarded as the queen of blues and was the winner of several beauty contests. Now she leads the quiet life of a shebeen queen in Mabopane. Thoko occasionally appears on stage or runs music workshops, but has mainly bowed out of public life and is now a housewife. Thandi, who tends to be the sexy Lena Horne type, woos the youth at cabaret shows and refuses to throw in the towel in spite of lack of opportunities.

Unlike their American counterparts who adapt to the tastes of each generation, our established musicians are generally stuck to the music of the 60s. Americans such as Roberta Flack and Aretha Franklin still sing their oldies, but have also come up with songs for the young. We have seen little of that here.

The "second generation" of township musicians, the Mara Louws and Count Judges, were into western music, and their contribution to SA sound was to incorporate township styles into it. They were able to break into the international scene much more fully than their predecessors, in a manner neither African nor Western.

After that era we saw a sharp move. Artists ceased to be creators or musicians. They churned out anything that would draw a clap. One of these artists says readily that his business is "opium music". It is sold cheap, and scores with people for whom anything will do as long as it is familiar, like an advertising jingle. "People want simple sounds they can hum. Regardless of meaning. A man identifies with Brenda or Yvonne. Try and sell him Nina Simone at twice the price, he won't be impressed."

The manager of a popular group expresses the same sentiments: "How do you tell a musician to come up with soul-searching music and end up poor? Nobody will buy that music. Whereas Yvonne Chaka-Chaka and Brenda Fassie move in the latest cars because of their music. Besides, white music is having the same problem. Their artists are suffering the same fate as our boys and girls — stars today and nothing tomorrow."

116

Maybe it is true that South African music is still looking for its authentic sound. A little while ago the in-thing was Shangaan or Venda music. People like Paul Ndlovu made a killing with Shangaan lyrics, and soon many artists went ethnic. Then came Paul Simon and Graceland.

Now there is the rise in African gospel music. Church choirs have bombarded studios with their rendition of hymns, but far from the old straightforward American style, more novel and indigenous. This has taken South Africa by storm. Some black artists have switched from pop to gospel. Some people claim that this music has attracted disillusioned politically active types, who have found in it a way of venting their frustrations, with SABC providing a platform.

Just as boerewors and pap merged to be regarded as a South African dish — so thoroughly that the Boers have forgotten that the pap side of that dish was ours to start with — who knows, some day the sounds coming from the Boland may merge with those of gospel and townsips in a colourful symphony of experiences to create the truly national love song we all yearn for.

22

Qualifying for manhood

THE demise of the dompas has brought some interesting views. One would have thought the scrapping of the pass would be a welcome event, after all the pass has been a thorn on black flesh. But there are those who feel that the acquisition of a pass was a measure of manhood.

Listening to the stories of people who came to the city in search of work one appreciates that it was more than officialdom at play. There were other forces and pressures these men and women had to deal with.

People who came to the city would stay with a relative or family friend. Sometimes it would also be a case of finding homeboys. No wonder there are townships where one will find people of the same background, like Pimville used to be known to be Basotho territory, Boksburg was Zulu and Alexandra Shangaan. That does not mean people from elsewhere were precluded from living in those townships. It was more a question of people being more comfortable with their own kind.

In many cases the incoming people depended for everything on the relative they lived with. He would be responsible for their upkeep. He would give them free board and lodging as well as bus fare to search for work. If his country cousin gets picked up in town without a pass he would have to pay either the bribe or whatever fine was imposed. The guardian would also scout around for whoever might be in the "pass fixing" business. And he would negotiate and pay.

In return the protégé would have to be obliging in many ways.

Some of the young chaps were well looked after but there are those who were not lucky to have loving uncles and aunts. They would be treated like Cinderellas. Those who survived became men with families, qualifying to be in Johannesburg with rights to rent or (lately) own homes. To them it was like a certificate of having triumphed over adversity. It was a badge of pride.

It should also be borne in mind that at times the host relatives were not intentionally mean to the relatives they had to accommodate. They had their own problems to cope with. It could also be that they were financially incapable of maintaining their own children let alone relatives. Lack of finances does strain relations and build up a lot of resentment.

I listened to men discussing their sons recently. They talked about how the present generation takes life and privileges for granted. "It is like we owe them a living," one of them said. He went on to say how he lived with his uncle and had to wash dishes while his cousins who were girls were lounging. He had to clean the stoep in the early hours while the rest of the family was still sleeping. Refusing meant he would be thrown out of the house, and not only that, his name would be erased from the house permit, and that would mean his influx status would be affected.

To this day those people hold members of the family in high or very low esteem, depending who did what to whom. You hear phrases such as "I hate Aunt so-and-so up to my dying days because she would not have me in her house permit". That person would not look deeper into his aunt's problem. The poor old girl might have been willing to have her niece or nephew's name appearing in the house permit but the husband would be against it. And how does she tell that to her relatives without exposing her husband as a mean guy? Other people show gratitude to an aunt or uncle after twenty years or more, for taking them in or for putting them on the house permit even without letting them stay in the house, so they had that stamp in their pass. Many relatives held the keys to other people's lives. Like Polish and Irish immigrants to America, immigrants to the city understood the traumas of being an alien.

So if one was made of weaker stuff, or came from a comfortable background, they would not tolerate suffering and would soon pack their bags and go back to the homelands. In a way, that was failure and some people are still reminded of that.

Having a pass with all the required stamps, or having one's name appear in a house permit, and particularly acquiring a 10(1)A stamp, was a status symbol. Some people used to sneer at those who were not lucky enough to qualify to be in Johannesburg. A woman with city rights could be in love with a guy from the homeland. Come breaking off time, it was quite common to hear the woman telling the world how lousy the man was, and "to crown everything, he does not even have a pass."

Apart from the pass fixing industry, which often operated in cahoots with officials, marriages of convenience took place.

Among the marriages I know, one stands out. A homeland girl had a boyfriend who was from Johannesburg and after discussion they agreed that they would be married out of friendship and in due course would part to find their real love matches, with the girl's status having been raised to urban citizen.

So without the rigmarole of wedding traditions, involving sending a delegation to the girl's home and paying lobolo, the couple went to the registrar's office, and after waiting the three weeks of the publication of the banns, they were legally married without their parents' knowledge.

For the girl, this was a great step towards Johannesburg rights. But the boy had something else up his sleeve. He started demanding his rights as a husband. The episode culminated in such a nasty tone, with the girl unwillingly pregnant and her parents demanding lobolo. And at that stage, the boy even refused to take her to the various offices and sign the papers she needed in order to get her qualifications. In the end, it was not only herself who was an illegal, but the unborn baby too. And there was no way she could have it born in a township clinic without a house permit. She was served with a 72-hours order to leave Johannesburg.

Despite all, she ended up living in the township and bringing up her beloved child there. She went on later to a real marriage and is now one of those who is proud of triumphing over the system.

It was quite sickening to find Johannesburg guys drinking themselves to death, refusing to work and spending the entire day basking in the sun and laughing at the so-called country bumpkins who had to dodge the police. Guys who qualified to be in the city would sit and watch as the police walked street to street escorting men in handcuffs whose only crime was a desire to be employed and lead a decent life. In many cases the qualified guys survived because of the power they could exercise over the bumpkins and the payments they could extort. Some of those clever guys are still unemployed. Today they envy those country bumpkins who slogged it and have carved a niche for themselves, even if it is only with pension schemes.

While it is true that there have been no fundamental changes for blacks, it is not true that the changes are cosmetic. For one thing, no longer does the appearance of a policeman spell trouble. One does not see men suddenly touching their inside pockets to check if they have remembered to transfer the pass into the jacket one is wearing. Also the urbanites who boasted with their permits have suddenly found they are no longer powerful. An unhappy relative can get a flat in town or rent a backroom or a shack and make a home for himself.

There is a school of thought which believes that born-and-bred Soweto people are non-achievers, having become spoilt by their privileges under the pass system. It is often remarked that the people who have scored great victories whether in business or in education are those who came from the outside. As foreigners who had to contend with a hostile Soweto, they have made something of their lives. Of course there are exceptions such as Mrs Marina Maponya, Caroline Mazibuko, and Makana Tshabalala. But if you look at the big success stories you find that the great majority were outsiders, and many of them came from origins where they would spend many hours a day walking miles to a poverty-stricken farm school. The Gabi Magomolas, Eric Mafunas and Reuel Khozas are not Soweto's sons.

I knew a girl from the Transkei who used to say to city girls: "I do not have a 10(1)A stamp in my reference book, but I have a job, a house, a husband and a child. You can only boast of your pass and the stamp."

Even in these days one of the greatest words in the township is still RT which stands for Registered Tenant. In a family squabble it is quite common for the head of the house to close arguments by saying "I am the RT and my word is final".

The other day a woman confided in her friend that she had had enough of her husband and was going to leave him for some time and go on "fed-up leave".

Her friend discouraged her from going away, pointing to her that there were too many unmarried women around who would move in as soon as she moved out. Her friend advised her to sleep in one of the rooms in the house.

Came evening, she took a few blankets and slept on the sofa in the living room. Around midnight she was awoken by her husband who demanded money for rent. "Look you can't squat in my living room. Give me money for rent. If you are my wife you should be in the bedroom or else pay me rent."

The joke is he is one of the rent resisters and has not paid his own rent for years. But then he is the RT, who is to challenge him?

23

The hatchet and the snow

———————— FEBRUARY 1989 ————————

ALTHOUGH Mzala's book, *Chief with a Double Agenda*, on Gatsha Buthelezi is fraught with sordid statements in its attempt to run him down, it is however a well researched document. In a country thirsty for unbiased history, it is a pity that Mzala's book is wrapped up in such hate that it defeats the purpose of destroying some of the myths the colonialist historians recorded. This reduces the possibilities of it ever becoming a respected African history book.

From the onset one is tempted to ask — who is Mzala? Why does he choose to hide in anonymity? Since he apparently lives in Lusaka with the ANC, he cannot be in fear of Inkatha. Does he lack the courage of his convictions so much that he gives in to a word which is especially meaningless even for a pseudonym? Mzala means cousin; what are we meant to read into that?

There is no doubt that the book is a work of an academic and historian. And yet from the very first page it poses strange questions. There is a very un-African feeling about much of the book. It is unusual in African tradition to slander even a worst enemy with such vitriol. And yet we should perhaps accept that African tradition is changing. One proof is the way that the book is being received around the townships of Durban and Pietermaritzburg. People there are directly affected by his reign and there his unpopularity is much greater than in Soweto or Lusaka, where it is an ideological or academic matter. Among literate people there, Mzala's book is the biggest excitement for years.

But there is information that is just not plausible. For instance

122

in going to great length to destroy Buthelezi's claim to be hereditary prime minister, Mzala says that a duty of Buthelezi's ancestor was to empty the queens' chamberpots. How can a Zulu write this? Does he know nothing of the sexism of Zulu men? There is no way that job could be done by males. Not even the uhlanya, the poor tattered halfwits who hung around at the court, and who at times would be killed when the inyanga decreed that some human organ was needed for muti to strengthen the king's regiment, could be assigned to such a degrading and demeaning position. Besides, the women lived in the isigodlo, the women's "own affairs department". The men came there for one reason only, and then left again. The idea of men being there as workers is completely ridiculous.

Those of us who have stayed here in South Africa have learnt that you cannot destroy someone by calling him names. It is what a person does that becomes his undoing. The people find the truth.

In Zulu tradition, the offsprings of a prince or princess are treated as royalty and called princes or princesses. Mzala, arguing that Gatsha should not be called "prince" ("mntwana"), says that this is not done even by the English. So what? Are the English the standards by which people measure themselves? Is it not enough that they are the only ones who can knight people? For as long as I remember, Brigadier Zulu of the Salvation Army used to be fondly addressed by most people in the church as "mntwana" and as far as I could trace his link with royalty, it was so remote that it didn't exist. But bearing the surname Zulu was enough; people regarded him as prince. The same goes for other people with that surname.

The monarch, King Zwelithini, no longer has political power. Unlike other countries, where kings have lost power because of natural dynamics, in our country the so-called "homeland" system was imposed and the normal process was distorted. The Xhosas revered the late King Sabata whose position was usurped by the Matanzimas. In Venda the main guys who held power were the Ramabulanas, who were displaced by Mphephu. And so is the story in Gazankulu. Where Mhlava should have led, instead Ntsanwisi overtook him. There are ever so many chiefs in BophuthaTswana, but the SA government brought a private citizen from Sophiatown to lead the BaTswanas. These changes were not by natural process, and they were not by choice of the people, who have never yet understood themselves to be freely able to vote as they wish. They were changes by choice of the SA government. Thus when Mzala questions Buthelezi's position as "leader of the Zulus", he has a point, but when he also says that Buthelezi is not recognised as chief of the Buthelezi clan, he is barking up the wrong tree.

Mzala says that Gatsha schemed to the chieftainship, stepping on his relatives' toes. He implies that Gatsha's elder brother Mceleli was meant to be chief. In fact this is not a one-way issue. It has been a subject of dispute. One traditionalist faction maintains that the first son is always the heir, but the other school alleges that the son of a princess takes precedence over an elder brother who is the son of a commoner. Even Mzala admits that the clan paid lobola for Gatsha's mother, but he seems unaware that this makes Gatsha's case very strong.

Mzala says that Mceleli has been banished to the northern Transvaal. I was intrigued by this statement and on investigating I found that Mceleli is actually employed as a security guard at Gatsha's official residence, Kwaphindangene.

To show Mzala's pettiness, he talks of Chief Buthelezi naming the commission that was conducted by Prof. Schreiner as the Buthelezi and not the Schreiner Commission. What is wrong with that? Does that affect the findings of the commission? We live in a country where those wielding power will name everything after them, from police stations to highways, bridges and tunnels.

Chief Buthelezi frequently makes reference to his stint in the ANC Youth League. Mzala obviously does not like this, because it gives Buthelezi some "relevance". Therefore he denies that Buthelezi was in the Youth League. I checked out with Mr Godfrey Pitje, a Johannesburg attorney and former chairman of the Youth League. He confirms that Chief Buthelezi was in the League. And so does AB Ngcobo, now exiled in London.

Putting aside the writer's passion to destroy Chief Buthelezi, the book gives a spellbinding analysis of black history up to the latter day.

Then comes Jack Shepherd-Smith with a well-written public relations job which manages to be bootlicking and patronising at the same time, entitled *The Biography*. To me it is always amusing to hear that Buthelezi is the leader of 6 million Zulus, in which I am included. When and where would he lead me? Jack Shepherd-Smith as usual relies on the big crowds which Gatsha used to pull at Jabulani Amphitheatre to show evidence of support in Soweto. In a country where our leaders are incarcerated or in exile, listening to a public political rally is an experience. Did that make him leader of all who went there? Does he lead the liberals whom he time and again addresses? Was he Alan Paton's leader? When Rev Jesse Jackson visited South Africa and had hundreds coming to listen to him, was he their leader? Is a leader not someone who speaks on behalf of followers? How can a homeland leader even think that he can solve our problems in the cities?

124

What can he say about rent hikes, child abuse, drugs and the problems giving township residents brain damage? I do not know a single Zulu in Soweto who looks on Gatsha as his leader.

Many Zulus take offence to the assumption from whites that because they are Zulu they support Buthelezi. No Mosotho or Xhosa will ever say when it comes up that I am Zulu "Oh, you belong to Gatsha" or some such thing, but most whites immediately say something of that nature. It is as if I met a Scot and when he asked me how my chief was, I replied: "how is your duke?" Many people have no ideological interest in Gatsha one way or the other, but are unhappy to be called "his people".

In KwaZulu the scene is different. There are genuinely honest followers of the Inkatha cause but there are also members who are there for expedience, especially at leadership level. For the ordinary person joining Inkatha is one of those things that one does without choosing, like paying taxes. A person cannot be sure of receiving a pension or vacancy or a site or many other things without an Inkatha card. Of course this is vehemently denied by the KwaZulu authorities, but for all their denials everyone who knows KwaZulu knows it is true.

While Mzala takes every opportunity to discredit Chief Buthelezi, Jack does the opposite. Mzala paints him snaking his way into politics, while Jack speaks of him being sought out by the likes of the ANC. Jack says that King Solomon wanted to honour Chief Buthelezi's father, and that is why he arranged that his sister "the comely young princess" should marry him. Mzala says that the princess was on the shelf.

Apart from different facts, the two authors choose different polls, with Mzala naturally using the polls which make Chief Buthelezi look pathetic and Shepherd-Smith using the other polls. Mzala does occasionally give Buthelezi some grudging credits, but Jack seems determined that his hero must be superlative in every single way, even to the way he sings and the way he acts, and seems to have scoured the dictionary for flattering adjectives. By the end, both books become obnoxious, with the bias turning one off. One wants to find the truth for the sake of the truth, and not for propaganda.

24

Living a lie, reaping a whirlwind

TWO years ago, when *Frontline* published information regarding the Mandela United Football Club, what was interesting was the reaction that followed. A great number of Soweto residents, especially from around Orlando West near the Mandela house, accused us of scratching the surface and not exposing all. Meanwhile politicians, including white liberals, accused us of supporting the government side, and some others said it was wrong to air black people's dirty linen to the white public.

The white media latched on to one part of the story — Mrs Mandela's new mansion — and ignored the issue of the football club. Perhaps it was easier to focus on the house as it stood there for everyone to see. Although both issues were already major topics of conversation in Soweto, black newspapers kept silent about the house as well as the football club.

Mrs Mandela summoned certain leading journalists to her house. She told them that we were agents of the system and they should publish that. They did not, knowing this as untrue, but kept in with her by running complimentary stories.

One liberal newspaper published a story portraying the Football Club as a haven for homeless boys, being harassed by the police. At that time residents of Phefeni in Orlando West were frantic with fear of their sons being press-ganged by the Football Club. Members of the club were openly walking around Soweto with machine-guns over their shoulders, and people in Soweto were mystified as to why the police were laying off.

All sorts of people urged me that I should leave home for a while, but on learning of the issue my neighbours insisted that I stay and their menfolk would keep watch. After a few days the watch fell away and the matter was forgotten.

The episode made us uneasy at the gap between the media picture of South Africa and the reality. White people, and some blacks from afar, thought that I was betraying the black cause. But in Soweto I was congratulated even by people from the ANC/UDF fold. Only a few had serious complaints, saying that no information which was bad for the struggle should be tolerated, whether true or not.

Now that the wheel has turned, it is sad to see the rush to descend like vultures, heaping all the blame on one pair of shoulders as if shunning her will solve the problems.

Winnie is just a woman who under normal circumstances would have been a woman like any other, carrying on with her profession and running her life like an ordinary mortal. But the illness of the system cast her into a role she could not handle, and now her downfall is treated as a reason for continuing that illness.

Blacks are walking with their heads down, feeling she has brought shame on us all. Many are told by white people: "It shows that you are better off with us ruling, because this is how you would be ruled otherwise." But the real problem is the system. If blacks were citizens with proper political structures, the whole affair would have been brought short long ago.

All along there has been hypocrisy in the treatment of Winnie. I have known people who have appeared in newspapers hugging her, including whites, to privately tell all sorts of stories. Of the people who are rushing to distance themselves from her, some have for years known of courts and punishments behind her walls, and when her neighbours went to the leaders to tell of the screams, the leaders said it was the work of the struggle. Some prominent people have played the role of assistant judges. Now they are saying it is wrong, but they said nothing when it was still supposed to be "the work of the struggle" and there was glamour in the people setting up rival courts to the regime's courts.

Headlines like "Fallen Idol" create the impression that blacks had revered the "Mother of the Nation". The fact is that this title is a mystery, and many black people have never known where it came from. Ever since it appeared it has been common to hear people scoffing, with phrases like "No, my mother is Mrs So-and-so". However, the title was made popular in the eyes of the outside world, which shows that if a small group of people set out with determination to create a lie, they can succeed.

127

The lesson is that if we wish to be understood, we must speak up in time, and not trail along with the lies until they crash upon us.

This is not the only lie we have lived with. The whole issue of black leadership needs a close look. At a recent seminar I was surprised to find that the speaker was a "black leader". This was a Soweto person who I had never heard of and who went ahead to tell the white audience that his own personal views were "what blacks think". No wonder the whites are confused about us, and we are confused about ourselves. How can anyone know who is a leader and who is not, when anyone with a black skin and a mouth can be a "black leader" if he says he is?

Many people have been calling for the government to unban the political movements not as a game to score points but as a genuine attempt to bring about stability. When the country was engulfed in blood and fire, we would have done anything to have leaders to speak to and ask some questions. When children sought "liberation now and education later", we wanted to be able to speak to leaders. When people's homes were gutted and their cars taken we wanted to know if that would bring us liberation. But with the movements banned there was nobody we could ask. What we saw was lawlessness and destruction, and how did the government react? It banned the few organisations that sought to intervene, and put emerging leaders into jails.

We are only beginning to reap the results of that era. The "Stompie" case is an example.

Who was Stompie? We are told that he left school at standard 2 and he could recite the Freedom Charter. This when some of our matriculants struggle with even the simplest of recitations such as "The Highwayman". We are told that he addressed a gathering at Wits University, carrying an attaché case. Where were the leaders then? Where were the men? Is the struggle a game, to be waged by children making spectacles of themselves for white amusement? We are told he was a general in charge of a 1 500-strong "children's army" in Tumahole. Knowing Tumahole as I do, I doubt that anyone could muster 1 500 children there for any purpose, and the idea of an "army" and a "general" with those images of order and discipline is simply ridiculous.

Watching little Stompie doing the "toy-toy" on TV, I only see a youngster being paraded by the big boys to depict a struggle that has become a plaything.

One cannot think of Stompie without experiencing a lump in one's throat. I very well remember a scene described to me the morning after SADF helicopters had raided the Wilgespruit centre in search of youngsters who had fled from Tumahole. The children had been chased all over the bush. Some were captured and others had their clothes torn by the trees. Shoes and all kind of clothing lay strewn all over the place.

This was the time when youngsters were formed into gangs to protect residents from eviction, and the gangs got out of hand. It was the time when the youngsters were feared and one dared not be against them. Stompie was part of that world. But whether they were doing good or bad, there is a terrible indictment on black parents, who stood by while the children fought their war and then terrorised them.

Some people blame Stompie's mother for his death, the argument being how could she carry on with her life not knowing where her son was. In normal times this would be unheard of. I know mothers who panic at 7 o'clock on a Saturday evening when they know their sons have gone to a matineé in town and can only make it home after 8 pm. But in our circumstances, who can blame Stompie's mother? We are reaping the fruits. We take refuge in blaming the system, but while we all know that the system is the root cause of the problem, we need to look too at our response.

When we were growing up, the struggle belonged to the people. We spoke of the ANC and the PAC. It was a time when the man in the street did not even bother to find out what difference lay in the two organisations.

After 1976, we saw a move from organisational struggle to that of individualist. Certain names became more prominent than others, and in particular the name of Nelson Mandela.

Previously, Mandela had been but one of the top rank of the ANC. His highest office had been Transvaal provincial president and his status had been no greater than Sisulu or Govan Mbeki. But now Mandela began to stand out alone and then in 1978 the Release Mandela Campaign installed him as the chief prisoner, to the extent that in a few years the others were by-the-ways.

How this happened is not clear, although there is a belief that a certain meeting was held where it was decided that there was a need to personify the struggle, and Mandela was chosen partly on the grounds that his wife was young and beautiful and would attract more attention than the motherly MaSisulu.

Whatever the truth may be, in the late 70s we watched Winnie ascend the throne and occupy it regally. When she was banished to Brandfort there was indignation, and when she returned, defying her banning order, that caused pride.

But then at first the local neighbourhood became concerned and then the concern stretched further. It is often said that Winnie's remark about matches and necklaces started her downfall, but that is only half true. Some worry already existed, and on the other hand, the matches remark did not at first create distress.

Many people at that time still perceived the necklace as a symbol of the struggle. I admit that I personally was at one time tolerant of the necklace. I saw it as the treatment that informers deserved. It was only after I saw a necklace case with my own eyes that I became furiously opposed to the use of murder in the struggle. I also did not at first realise how easily the weapons of murder and violence become abused. Even now, whilst totally hating all violence and all man-made death, I still believe that we have a legitimate war to fight for our liberation. I cannot bring myself to say categorically that it is wrong to use violent means to procure liberation. I am not able to reconcile these things. I would give anything to see liberation come about peacefully, but I cannot see how. So I remain confused and distressed about the issue of violence, and there are many people in the same boat.

When Winnie talked of matches, I did not at first feel revulsion, but disquiet. In the townships many people were saying that the necklace had been one thing while it was used by youths. There was a feeling that it was barbaric, but the barbarism was explained away by the great need for success in the struggle. But when it came from Winnie's mouth, it seemed that barbarism was now being legitimised and institutionalised. Winnie's remark changed the attitude towards the necklace, with the disquiet growing to revulsion over a period of months, until the time came that almost every black person is bitterly ashamed that the necklace ever appeared, which is the situation today.

Meanwhile, other things were brewing. Some people tried to speak seriously to Winnie, but got nowhere. In one case a group of women had formally arranged a meeting. When they got to Winnie's house, having dressed to the nines and prepared themselves over days, Winnie greeted them and then left in her car, saying she would be back in a moment. They sat there for half the day without a cup of tea, and Winnie never re-appeared.

All this sort of thing was happening against a background where rumours had been rife for a long time. Soweto people are a very conservative lot. And they have long memories. People have always looked askance when a pretty young wife displaces an older first wife, and in addition there had always been a large number of specific rumours which, whether true or not, are widespread.

Then when the violent era was dying down there came the period of good works, when children were cleaning up their areas and building parks. This was a welcome time, although even then people were sometimes forcibly required to donate. Then the park story faded away and in came football clubs which were to exalt heroes.

The Sisulu FC was set up in Orlando and the Motswaledi FC in Mzimhlophe, named after Elias Motswaledi, a local activist who is on Robben Island, as well as some associated with trade unions. These were short-lived but the Mandela FC took root. Mrs Mandela bought uniforms for them and made them comfortable in her house. Rapidly it became evident that this was not a normal football club, and in fact it seems that they were only ever fixtured for one game, which was a game against the Delmas trialists arranged by overseas TV, and banned because it was scheduled for Mandela's birthday.

Even at the beginning, parents were concerned that their children were being taken up in the football club, and said that the children there were toughs and delinquents rather than football players. Some sent their sons to homeland relatives, to keep them out of the club's orbit.

The club thought it had the freedom of Phefeni and later Soweto. The first big clash was with Daliwonga school students when the club told them to vacate a ground they were using. A fight ensued which ended with the students running away when guns were produced. After this, hostilities set in, culminating in Daliwonga students burning down the Mandela house two years later after a rape incident.

Meantime the club was growing, acquiring vehicles such as a minibus donated by an Embassy and money donated by Winnie's white friends. On occasion vehicles were taken from township residents. Club members accompanied Winnie everywhere, one even attending her at university, the joke in the townships being that he should get an honorary degree for the time spent there. People were saying South Africa must be the only country whose liberation could be fought by a football team.

One thing about Soweto is that it has certain people who are pillars. These may not be political heavies or big shots but they are nevertheless the pride of the townships, respected for their personality rather than for committee involvement or any such thing. Nobody messes with them.

Bra Billy Leballo is one such man. He runs a florist shop. Soft spoken and witty, he stands six foot six and can tell you one or two stories about Sophiatown. He was never involved in politics or gangsterism but he is not a moegoe. When Western Native township was moved he bought a house in Dube and there he lived for many years.

At some stage Billy's wife became an "umzabalazo lady", a lady of the struggle, and a friend of Winnie's. When a divorce action came up, the football club arrived at Billy's house and told him to vacate it for his wife to take over.

Those who know the Sophiatown lot know that you do not tamper with those blacks. Word got around and there was a hush of expectancy. But Bra Billy, who is now pushing 60, decided the matter was for the law. He brought an interdict and people watched with interest. They thought that the club was going to be checked. Then Bra Billy lost the case. People did not know what legal technicalities there may have been, but saw the case as showing that Winnie was above the law. There was a feeling that people were dealing with something larger than they had thought, and hostile talk became rampant.

Then there was the Seheri case. Seheri was a ANC cadre staying at Winnie's house. He suspected a youth of stealing a scorpion machine pistol at a shebeen and tracked the youth to his home where he shot him dead with an AK47 rifle in his mother's bedroom.

In court there was evidence that the AK47 which Seheri used had been found by police in Zindzi Mandela's bedroom. People thought that now the whole business was going to be blown wide open, the norm being that if arms are found in the house the police will round up everybody as well as friends and relatives, and no-one will sniff free air again for a long time.

However, strangely enough in this case the law seemed to be going about it in a most unusual way. The householder did not even give evidence. A lawyer tells me that this is correct in law, because the defendant had made admissions about the guns, but it seemed very strange to people in Soweto. The matter caused a loss of confidence in the judiciary. It seemed that according to the rules of politics, not everyone was equal in the eyes of the law.

Another story began back in the days of street committees, when Masabatha was killed near her house on a Friday afternoon by a gang of 21 males, who were openly seen and known to many nearby residents. Masabatha was a model and beauty queen and had also been an activist who had served five years. She was prominent in street committee work and it is widely believed that her committee had aroused jealousies among others who believed that her street was meant to be part of their territory.

Some time later a youth, Tholi Kenneth Dlamini, a son of a well-known Phomolong family, defected from the comrades he had been associating with to return to school and his previous hobby of ballroom dancing. His brain was blown out à la Al Capone style with a Makaroff machine gun. People round Orlando West were distressed about this whilst also saying "while we feel sorry at his death, we have not forgotten that he was one of those who killed Masabatha".

A further incident involved the burning of the house of one of the artists who sang in the government's "Brighter Future" propaganda song. This visit was followed by a condolence visit from people who were believed to have done the burning, which caused astonishment.

In the light of this history the events which have been publicised in the last few weeks have not come as a surprise in Soweto. If you ask people around Orlando West, most will tell you that they cannot understand why it took so long.

Looking back, we at *Frontline* can also feel guilty that we did not speak more clearly before the chaos reached its pitch. If in the end it turns out that the death of Dr Abubakar Asvat was also somehow connected, we can feel worse because there was one of the truly saintly human beings of our times. However we referred three times to what was going on, and if we did not (and still do not) pull out all the stops it is because we are not detectives whose business is to present courtroom evidence. Nor are we a newspaper, but a background magazine. We thought the newspapers would pursue the issues, but all that happened is that we were accused of waging a lone political vendetta for ulterior motives.

On the face of it, it seems that the result is another blow against peace and confidence and the things we want but do not achieve in South Africa. But looking deeper it may be that Stompie and the others did not die in vain. They may have taught us lessons: that when we live lies we reap whirlwinds, and that if there is to be order in our land, it will come when the leaders can be called to account by the ordinary decent people who are currently battling to preserve their morality through the disasters which white rule produces.

While the violent aspects of the affair now come to the fore, a postscript still awaits. This is to do with the three houses which Mrs Mandela now has in Soweto.

When the first house, Nelson Mandela's own home, was gutted by Daliwonga students, community leaders promised that it would be rebuilt. It was rebuilt by a company owned by one of those leaders, who is now complaining that his company has not been paid. Meanwhile, questions are being asked about how he came to acquire a building company, since he has been an activist since the days of Steve Biko. He has been chairman of several political projects awash with foreign funds, and it is suggested that in the interests of defusing suspicions he should lay out his books for scrutiny in the way that politicians in democratic countries are required to do.

The second house, the palace now called the "Soweto Sun", was built on four sites for which the stand owners were paid in cash. Who owns the house is unclear. At first the idea was that a trust would be responsible on behalf of the nation, pending Mandela's release. But then Winnie wanted the house in her own name, on the grounds that she had nothing after her years in the struggle. It is understood that Mandela had not been keen, even when he thought the house was a R300 000 job, and had told Winnie that if she needed more space she should buy the house next door to her existing house, and that when he found out that the new mansion was being built, with costs up more than two-fold, he expressed dissatisfaction.

Additionally there was uncertainty about what money was Winnie's and what was the trust's. Aside from royalties from Winnie's book *Part of My Soul*, there were large donations, including one from Harry Belafonte. A black company was commissioned to build the house, and now the company has gone under, with about R100 000 still owed on the house. The house, now completed, sits empty, and it is said that there are moves to turn it into a clinic.

The third house, in Diepkloof Extension, is the house where Mrs Mandela now lives. The owner had put it on the market expecting about R150 000, but was offered much more in cash, apparently by the American adventurer Brown who had some arrangement with the Mandela family. However, at just that time the arrangement was changed or terminated, so now when the seller goes to Brown he says go to Winnie, and when he goes to Winnie she says Brown is meant to handle it.

Now that the wraps are being lifted, there is no knowing where it will end. Currently the fashion is to load everything onto Winnie's head and to take all she says as evidence that she is out of touch with reality.

When it is all over, I do not think it will be that easy. The sodomy story which Mrs Mandela has brought up will not seem so bizarre. I know nothing about the particular individuals she has referred to, but I can say that an issue regarding children being sodomised at places where they have sought refuge, is coming up. Here is another lie we have been living, letting this remain under cover. Further, I doubt that the story about infiltration by agents provocateurs will be laughed at in the long run. We will see. In the meantime, all we learn is that sweeping dirt under the carpet does no good, and that we truly need a fundamental change in the way this country is run.

25

Misdirected advertising

―――――――― JUNE/JULY 1989 ――――――――

THERE is a deodorant advert on television where a white guy, clapping eyes on a sweet young lass, rushes to buy a bouquet of flowers to give to her. Well and good but now there is an identical black version and I must say it is most unconvincing.

This is not because black people do not like or buy flowers, but not in this way. Black men just don't do that sort of thing. Not only do they not buy flowers for their girls or lovers but there is no way a black man can buy something for a stranger. And that has nothing to do with being miserly. Just as whites hardly ever accost and talk to strangers. You can see them in the bus or train. They rather bury their faces in the newspapers than talk to fellow travellers.

White men do not leer and shout appreciative remarks to a woman walking down the street. Black men excel in that. In fact time was when that was tradition. That was how men showed their interest to girls.

The most beautiful unwritten poetry is used by black men on women. For instance there was a popular phrase which went something like: the one who has killed a buck has not roasted it, if he has roasted it he has not eaten it, and if he has eaten it he has committed a crime. (Noseyishayile akakayosi, nosoyosile akakayidli, noseyidlile udle icala.)

The point was that it was considered very unscrupulous for a young Zulu to woo someone else's girl, so a guy had to work out other ways of making advances to a woman without appearing a jerk.

In particular it was taboo to approach a girl who was bespoken by someone of your own clan, so when a Zulu man had his eye on a woman his opening line would be: Ntombi uthanda kwabani? (Girl, which family have you chosen?) Mark, the question is not who the girl's lover is, but what his surname is. Whoever was interested in a girl had to make sure that he was not eyeing his "brother's" girl.

That was how important family names were. There are hundreds of thousands of Khumalos or Nkomos, but if the girl answered "Khumalo" then any Khumalo immediately laid off, regardless that he might only be related to that Khumalo through an ancestor ten or twenty generations back.

This custom has changed dramatically in the space of just a few years. In the old days, you did not need to know who someone bearing your name was or where he or she came from. Anyone who bore that name was your brother or sister. Today you hear people say although we share the same surname, he is not my relative.

Of course a lot of that has come from the Western influence of nuclear families. But there is also another explanation. When people from beyond the Limpopo came to South Africa, they had to apply for Reference Books. As aliens they would not qualify for South African status bearing their real names. So they adopted local names, especially Ndlovu and Mnisi. These people knew nothing of the history of the names they had adopted.

It was not long when one heard comments such as "No, he is a Rhodesian Ndlovu" or "a Kenyan Gule". However, a few surnames have stood the test of time, such as Khumalo. To this day the Khumalos regard Ndebele Khumalos as their brothers. Any Khumalo person will say "There was one Khumalo from whom we all came."

The Basotho chaps are even funnier. Instead of paying attention to the woman, they go on and on about who they are, the family tree and all. The purpose being to imply: dumb would be a woman who turns down the son or grandson or great-grandson of so-and-so, who achieved this or that distinction.

The modern-day educated executive tends to be inhibited. He will not woo or compliment a woman passing by. But the ordinary guy takes it for granted to make comments to the opposite sex, and the woman does not feel insulted. In fact even "high-class" women will say that their days are made by a group of men seated at the back of a lorry. These unsophisticated labourers will go wild and say the funniest things such as "dudlu, nongenabaskidi uyangena emakethe" (one does not need a basket to get to the market) or "nongena butcher uyayidla inyama" (it is not only those who own butcheries that eat meat).

Everyone knows that they don't mean what they say and if a woman took them up on their bold offers they would probably blush with embarrassment. It's all done for fun. It is sad that this kind of thing is dying as people become more aware of themselves and as new classes emerge which find it infradig to behave in the ways of their fathers.

But to verify my comments about black men buying flowers for their lovers, not that I disapprove, I watched the reaction of a group of teenagers when the commercial was on. I remarked "Oh, what a gentleman." It was so funny when one said "Isilima" (fool) and another said "Imbongolo" (ass).

I could not visualise any of the boys rushing off to get a bunch of flowers for a girl. It's not because it is vulgar or tasteless. Black boys do buy Christmas cards and perfumes for their girls. Black men do shower their women with all sorts of presents but not with flowers.

Even those who have spent years abroad and have become black Europeans have not come back and bought flowers for their girls. But then the world of advertising is a world of white men selling things to blacks. It is sometimes oblivious, and perpetuates myths.

Another example is the mealie meal commercial which tells us that to be a man and be strong you have to eat pap. The scene is of a labourer enjoying a dish of pap and meat. No harm in that, but it gains a strange echo in the changing township environment.

The idea comes across that pap is for labourers and that if you live in Diepkloof "Expensive" and work for the bank you do not need to eat that stuff, and this ties in with the general belief that the people in the rich areas can't manage to eat properly.

The belief is that those people spend all their money on their bond and flashy appearances and that they only eat well when they go back to their humble parents in the old townships.

Way back at the creation of Dube, the first middle-class township, the story was that Dube people ate offal which was delivered at night so the neighbours would not see.

At that time offal was the cheapest meal. Today it is regarded as a kind of delicacy and a proof of blackness, like pap is to the exiles in Europe and America. (To these people, funnily enough, boerewors and biltong also bring tears to the eyes and are treated with great ceremony, although back home in the townships no black person even looks at biltong.)

From then on I suppose that most of the skinder-stories about the habits of the middle-class blacks were fabrications by jealous people. Even today it is common for the poor people in the old townships to believe that the rich people in the new townships label their foodstuffs to be eaten on certain days of the week. Mind you, maybe that is true after all. What definitely is true is: Woe unto the maid who eats an apple which little Thabo was to take in his "scarf tin" (lunch pack) to school.

In this situation it seems to me to be dangerous to label a particular kind of food as "for labourers". Some perverse and unintended consequences follow.

Africa's way

I was invited to an international conference about South Africa. As everyone knows, these conferences mean little in terms of what is actually going on here at home, but one goes anyway because somebody is paying the bill and it is a pleasure to see the world and meet people. However, I was disturbed when one of the delegates, a cabinet minister from an African country, spoke of solving problems the "African way". The more he spoke of "the African way", the more worried I became.

Some of us who are yearning for our liberation have reservations about this phrase "the African way". We wonder whether it is used as a disguise for the fact that liberated Africa is a very long way from where everybody wanted it to be, and where people thought it would go to when liberation arrived.

What does "the African way" mean? Does it mean the demise of order and rise of chaos? Does it mean the replacement of an orderly but unjust white domination by a disorderly and equally unjust clique domination? That the hope of liberty, fraternity and prosperity is dashed?

Since the time of liberation, Africa has acquired an instant "African tradition" of sacrificing truth for ideology. No wonder that journalists are unable to give us a true picture of what is going on in their countries. No wonder most African writers are in exile.

One African writer, addressing a group of South African writers, warned us to write now because in a black-run South Africa we may find it difficult.

On the plane home I found myself sitting for part of the way next to a Kenyan. At first he praised and applauded me as his sister from the oppressed South, but as the flight wore on and he mellowed, he finally said: "stop looking forward to your liberation because once you have got it you will go backward. We know."

For me this was a terrible shock. It does not really sway me, because I demand and insist upon my total liberation and total citizenship of my country, and until I have achieved that I do not care what happens thereafter. Nonetheless this Kenyan made me realise that we do not need liberation in name alone, we need liberation which is real.

I have over the years pondered the irony that while the Botha regime stands with an axe over freedom, and is world-famous for its oppression, I have cousins in other parts of the continent who cannot say even a tenth of what I say in public.

The trouble is that the South African government becomes complacent. It points to hunger and corruption in neighbouring countries and uses this to justify white rule. I can never accept white rule. As long as they make me an inferior being I do not have the luxury to work on what it means to make liberation real. I have to be prepared to swallow whatever kind of liberation comes up, lousy as it may be.

Second-class Africans

We as blacks find it most distressing that we cannot travel freely in Africa. One would have thought that because one is black and therefore a victim of apartheid, our black brothers would be sympathetic to us. One would have hoped that since the continent is now black governed, it would be easy for black South Africans to travel intra-Africa. Instead it has become worse.

It is very humiliating to watch South African whites who carry British passports in their inside pockets being able to travel all over Africa. They do not even need visas to visit these countries, while we do. It is said that this is for reasons of "precaution", and the fact is that the governments of Africa are hardly bothered about white travellers. They see these travellers as bringing trade and commerce and as no threat, whereas black strangers are always suspected of having some involvement with some or other dissident movement.

For Africans it is easier travelling around Europe than Africa. For one, should a black South African experience a problem with his passport, he will at the worst be sent on the first flight back to South Africa. But if the same happens in an African state then I am afraid the consequences are too ghastly to contemplate. He will be suspected of being a spy, and the rest everybody knows.

Baring it all

Is it the hangover from colonial rule, or why is it that each time a statesman from Europe visits Africa everything comes to a standstill? There is a guard of honour at the airport and a huge display of paraphernalia, fanfare and song. And yet when African leaders visit Europe it is business as usual, with just a little bit of discreet ceremony.

When Martti Ahtisaari arrived in Windhoek as the UN representative, a bevy of girls danced, baring it all in his honour.

Why is Africa doing such silly things, being an amusement? If Ahtisaari wants bums and tits let him go to a show. If not, let's show dignity.

26

The common customs of blacks and boers

EVERYBODY has heard the story that "the blacks favour the boers over the English." What is the truth of this story? It is not a simple matter. The English naturally like to think it is nonsense. They see themselves as the gentle ones, to whom the blacks turn with relief after the harshness of the Afrikaner. The Afrikaners love the story. They see themselves as entrusted by God to be guardians of the blacks, and they like to think there is a special bond between themselves and the blacks, which the English and the outside world do not understand.

Personally, I have all my life had an English orientation, and have had little to do with boers. However, I am time and again struck by hearing black people making judgments about the relative merits of the boers and the English.

For example, it is often said that the English will grin and make you believe they like you, but when the need comes up they will ditch you lightly. It is said that the boers will not hire you if they do not like you, or that if the chemistry is not right they will fire you forthwith. But if they like someone, they will move heaven and earth for him. With the English, the argument is that they will keep you on even if they cannot stand you, smiling all the time and being polite and decent while privately they are looking for a replacement. As soon as they find one, they will terminate your services without bother.

While this is obviously a gross generalisation it is a common generalisation. It applies not only among humble people like domestic servants or labourers, but it is also known in "middle-class" circles.

I have a friend who reluctantly took a job with an Afrikaans company, which is shunned by many blacks because of its identification with the government and Afrikaner political behaviour. Yet my friend is now a strong defender of this company. He says that the blacks there are treated with more respect than is known in liberal companies which have public images.

Some time ago one of their black executives was involved in a nasty accident. His Afrikaner boss and colleagues did not for one moment forsake him. They made sure he was booked at the best hospital, and they personally spoke to the doctors and monitored his progress. When the guy came to from his coma, the first person he saw was a boer colleague. The company did not just want him for window-dressing; they took a real interest in him.

When this guy was telling this story, one of the people present was a black woman who works in a high-profile liberal firm. She then told her own story in contrast. She said that she had once been at a glittering function, escorted by one of the well-known Soweto big shots. Her own MD came over to meet the big shot, and that was the first time he met her, his employee. He had not known what her name was, even though she was meant to be one of the top-level black success stories which are supposed to show the firm's commitment to a happy South African family.

Then there is the woman who went to an Afrikaans advertising agency. She too went there with little enthusiasm, because she couldn't find a place in a "respectable" agency, but she has now changed her views. When she went on maternity leave they threw a party for her and a baby shower. They visited her at the hospital, paid her whole medical aid premium while she was on leave, and, most important in these times of unemployment, they did not hire anybody for the months that she was away on maternity leave. They survived on freelancers.

She argues that in the Afrikaner setting there is a great deal of consideration for people, perhaps because the culture is less "high-powered" than the American-influenced pattern of the English companies, where the bottom line is all that counts and people are only wanted for their contribution to profits. She speaks of the MD stopping to talk to her, enquiring after her children, whose names he remembered, while also telling her stories about his grandson. These things make her feel at home and comfortable, so that when acquaintances now raise their eyebrows on learning that she works for an Afrikaans company, she no longer feels apologetic — she gives them short shrift.

She also mentions one small way in which she is more at home in the Afrikaans environment, which is that colleagues are not expected to pretend to be intimates. They call each other by their surnames, with the formal titles "Meneer" or "Mevrou". She finds this in keeping with her own African traditions, where respect is shown by putting a prefix before a name. In the English companies, she says, you at first think the people are all amazingly close friends because they call each other by first names from the word go, and even by pet forms of their first names, but then you realise that this is quite hollow. When the time comes they just stab each other in the back and then forget about the person who a week earlier had sounded like their best friend. She says black culture and Afrikaans culture have more in common than you think when just looking at the political buggerup. I think she has a point. For example I have yet to hear of a boer complaining about a black woman breastfeeding a baby in public, yet I have often heard English people go on about "animal behaviour" and "primitive customs" as if breastfeeding was a sin.

What is the woman supposed to do when her child is hungry? Must she rush around frantically hunting for a black public toilet, and then go and sit furtively in the cubicle? No, she does what is natural. She sits graciously and harmlessly on the pavement, and she offers the baby the sustenance which God provided for the purpose.

Then you get English-speaking gentlemen going purple with disgust, and saying here is proof that blacks are inferior beings. To me it is they who are displaying inferiority. If they want to go panic-stricken at the sight of a natural part of human anatomy, that is their problem. We are above such things.

Moreover, the same Englishman who will object to the breast being put to its natural purpose as a life-giving machine, will not turn a hair at the sight of "with-it" English youngsters kissing and cuddling at bus-stops or on park benches, and making the most intimate of intentions very clear indeed. That is the behaviour which we blacks find despicable; that is what should rightfully be a private activity. There too is something we have in common with the boers.

Now I bring this subject up because of what I have been noticing since TV presenter David Hall-Green made a notorious comment about a black woman who had apparently been on his show. He said, "I bet she has 14 children and all by different men."

This comment caused great anger and it still causes anger, because there is Hall-Green still sitting on his show, just as if nothing happened. Where is all the "respect" and the "new South Africa" we are always being told about?

Anyway, what was interesting was how this comment was treated as "typical of the English". What people were saying in the taxis was that only an English-speaking person could say that, as the Afrikaners know better. Unlike the know-all English writing theses about the barbaric African tribes, the Afrikaner has lived and worked shoulder to shoulder with the Africans and could not throw out such an insult.

One woman was at a presentation where one of the whites said Hall-Green was justified. She said an Afrikaner took cudgels on her behalf. He told the group how no black father could condone a teenager falling pregnant. He said that if a girl in a village fell pregnant, her father would be expected to pay a fine to cleanse the village of the scourge brought about by his daughter. In turn, the boy's father would also do his bit by paying damages to the girl's home. He tried to explain to the ignorant that there was no free-flowing sex in black society.

Well we all know how the structures in our societies have fallen under the pressures of our impotence, but that Afrikaner hit the nail on the head. We blacks have a moral code that is at least as intact as any other culture I know of — why is it that we are the ones who do not need orphanages and adoption agencies? — and we do not need unfounded insults from people who know nothing about us.

27

The triumph of English

IT'S lunchtime in the city. Three black teenage girls discard a fish-and-chips packet on the pavement and walk away. A street cleaner reprimands them. They brusquely tell him in English that it's his job to clean the streets, not theirs.

Listening nearby is a middle-aged woman. She calls to the girls and tells them it's bad enough to be rude to a man who could be their grandfather, even worse to address him in English. They tell her that English comes naturally; she tells them how disgusted she is. If being educated means adopting foreign languages to be rude to old people, the woman says, she's glad she's not educated.

And so it goes in South Africa: the continuing dispute over language.

For blacks, the use of English has always been a point of controversy, with fashions changing frequently from one concern — that our children need to be as competent in English as possible — to another, which is that we'll lose our identity and way of life.

As more black children attend white schools, the debate is becoming fierce. One fear is that the vernacular will fade away. Perhaps a bigger fear is that the children will adopt inferior foreign customs along with English, such as the habit of disrespect that seems to be flowing everywhere that American television reaches.

Attorney Chris Mokoditoa, once banned, sums up this attitude: "I have heard a child from one of those private schools saying, 'Granny, you are stupid.' I have nothing against the use of the language, but only if the child still knows her place in society."

The SABC's black television channels have added to the controversy, with their ever-changing language policies. Initially, the channels stuck rigidly to black languages, sometimes to ridiculous lengths. They would use words — such as *umabonakude*, for *television* — that nobody in real life ever uses.

Viewers found the "pure" vernacular to be unrealistic, arguing that TV should acknowledge that all black languages now include a good deal of English. Many complained that the SABC bosses should be more flexible and at least use English when the context called for it.

Today, there's plenty of English on TV 2 and TV 3. As often as not, all-black talk shows are carried out in English. So there are new complaints: that black languages are being shortchanged. It seems the SABC can't win.

The complaints are reasonable, since most blacks do not understand English — or at least not TV English, which is spoken at a rapid-fire rate. When the black channels were introduced in January 1983, there was much said about how the government was showing great respect for our languages and dignity. We were given two hours of viewing. This has now shrunk with the addition of TV4, with its white fare like cricket. So the non-English-speaker has even less to hear from his black brother on the box.

In his daily life, he also now hears more English than ever. Black political rallies and commemorations are conducted in English, and only the songs remain ethnic. Funerals are regularly in English, as are the messages on the wreaths and the inscriptions on the tombstones.

Strangers visiting black cemeteries could come out thinking that while blacks and whites live separately they are buried together. There are more tombstones with "Rest in Peace" written on them than "Lala Ngoxolo" or "Robala Kakgotso." Even when the deceased knew no English and hardly anybody at the graveside can speak it, the mourners will still bring their English wreaths and the priest will speak at least a bit of English as a sign of status.

There are those who think blacks who use English with fellow blacks are displaying a colonised mentality thinking that English makes them middle class and refined.

Others, just as adamant, argue that the age of the vernacular is over and that if we are to achieve prosperity and success, we'll have to adopt English.

Not that English is without its problems. One is that some kids see English as the sole requirement for success.

Says Soweto school principal Tom Cube: "If a student is good in English and thus assumes that he is intelligent, he is heading for a problem. English alone can't see one through school or through life.

But if he uses his command of English to acquire a better understanding of issues, then he will score." Cube encourages his pupils to speak English.

Young professionals stir animosity when they speak English at gatherings where the elderly cannot be expected to understand. Some of the elderly are outraged by the show of disrespect.

But other grannies and uncles are delighted to hear a junior family member rattling off in English, though they don't understand a word. They applaud his prowess, viewing it as an achievement the whole family can be proud of. They hear the English flowing over them and presume it to be full of wisdom, like Catholics at the old Latin services.

But there can always be strong resentment. A domestic worker, whose own English is not bad, says it's despicable to fail to be proud of your own language.

How does she greet strangers? "I approach them in Zulu, and if they answer in Sotho or Tswana I switch to it. If they answer in English, I assume that they are not South Africans and will speak in English. But if it turns out that they are South Africans from the 'Excuse Me' or 'High Sos' (High Society) set, then I will straight away revert to Zulu. There is no way I can speak to a fellow African in English."

It's not only blacks who are affected by the tide of English. How many young Indians speak their vernacular? They speak English. One young Indian told me his home language was Gujerati, which he couldn't even spell. He said his parents spoke Gujerati to themselves and their generation, but English to the youngsters. "And for us youngsters among ourselves, it's English all the time." He finds no resentment in South Africa but was treated with hostility when visiting India. "There, people do not want someone of my complexion to speak only English."

Meanwhile, Afrikaans is dying as the language of young coloureds. They speak Afrikaans at home to their parents but English among each other.

Even among white Afrikaners, we see the beginning of the end. Look at the names of young Afrikaans children. For every Koos or Hettie, you'll find 10 Charmaines or Steves. And it seems there's even more English interspersed in a normal Afrikaans conversation than there is in township talk.

Natural evolution will soon bring us to the point where children across South Africa will converse to their grandparents in English without blinking. And yet black South African children born in exile usually speak the languages of their native land. Sometimes, more

Zulu is spoken at the homes of exiles in Europe than at the homes of their brothers in Soweto or Durban.

Pauline Gule, a researcher with advertising agency Young and Rubicam, explains. "People in exile feel their languages are threatened, and a home language is like an umbilical cord binding them to their motherland," she says. "But back at home, you know that whether you or I speak to our friends and children in English all day long, there is no way our black languages can disappear. We interact with other people all the time in a black language: in the shops, at the bus-stops, at the sports stadium, everywhere."

Business executive Sej Motau, a former *Pretoria News* journalist, maintains that English is the language of liberation — a cry heard often in Namibia these days.

"We need to break out," Motau says. "We need to use English as a vehicle for communication and as an instrument for liberation. It frees one from the confinement of thinking like a Zulu or a Mosotho.

"Also, African languages with their cumbersome traditions tend to be circumlocutious, whereas English gets to the point. Our languages were good for the ox-wagon days. These days, we need English for practical reasons. Imagine a meeting conducted in African languages. How many would we use and which would we leave out and why?"

Adds Motau: "English is identified with positive things in our lives. I think more clearly when I use English, and I reach more people with it. Those who say the use of English is snobbish need the shackles of oppression removed from their minds. Their problem is their own inferiority complex. They can relax. Knowing English does not make anyone a better human being."

Motau's view faces much opposition. Communications executive Sandile Memela of Ogilvy & Mather says it's a "nice rationalisation," an attempt to suppress our guilt over having forfeited our mother tongues.

"We use English to make social statements — to show that we have sat behind desks and to distinguish ourselves from the unschooled and illiterate, who include our own parents," says Memela. "We use it to kill ourselves and our identity, of which we are secretly ashamed."

Whatever the rights and wrongs, the war is already won.

English will be the undisputed lingua franca in South Africa within a few years, and many of us may still see the day when it becomes the home language of most of the population.

It will be good if this evolves naturally and with general contentment, rather than the issue of language being covered with political implications — as so much in South Africa is.

28

In Soweto, the glowing embers

PEOPLE in the townships are meeting on various platforms to talk about growing lawlessness, but political and personal rivalries plague the issue. Nobody can agree on how to tackle the problem. And while the elite talk, the fabric of black communities is fraying. Unless we act, we're heading for a repeat performance of the 1986 chaos.

Recently, many of Soweto's professional and middle-class "establishment" met at the Dube YWCA to assess the Nation Building campaign, launched by *The Sowetan* newspaper to rebuild collapsed community structures. Strong hostility was expressed towards the Nation Building concept, which is often scoffed at as "Circulation Building" in middle-class circles.

Eugene Nyati, the chief counsel for the prosecution, damaged his case by making personal attacks on Aggrey Klaaste and Sam Mabe, the editor and assistant editor of *The Sowetan*. But Nyati also put his finger on the main point at issue. He said it is false for Nation Building to claim to be apolitical because being apolitical means supporting the status quo.

Nyati accused Klaaste of taking the line of "seek ye economic freedom and the rest will fall into place." He says this line misleads the masses into thinking they can become economically empowered without political clout. He says it's no accident that the Afrikaner first sought political power to become an economic force.

Nyati feels *The Sowetan* has rushed into the Nation Building campaign without thinking it through.

Many speakers rose from the audience to say they were all in favour of building the nation but had problems with the implementation of the campaign. Most said it is wrong to claim to be apolitical though maybe right to be nonpartisan. Some see no need for yet another organisation to be formed along Nation Building lines, claiming there are already too many organisations.

Some people made it clear that they resented Klaaste and Mabe for having made the concept "their baby," and argued that the concept has to be broadened and removed from *The Sowetan*.

The question of what the "nation" is came in for debate, with a Port Elizabeth delegate complaining that Soweto people seem to think Soweto is a nation, and others saying as a white-owned newspaper *The Sowetan* has no role in building the black nation. A woman felt Nation Building should start by addressing the problems facing families before getting on to national issues. She said black women are usually left to raise the children alone while the men go drinking.

The debate was uncomfortable, especially when delegates accused Klaaste — a Xhosa of aristocratic blood — of felonies like tribalism, by writing of leaders such as Mandela and Biko as Xhosas and his clansmen. The protagonists added little to our understanding of what exactly Nation Building is, which didn't exactly help matters. We have been seeing the phrase for a year and still do not know what it consists of.

The last speaker, Ramsey Ramokgopa of Funda Centre, calmed fraying emotions by refocusing attention on the dire need to regenerate confidence and order in black communities, something everyone can agree on.

Ramokgopa also criticised the tendency of black organisations to allow leadership to remain in the hands of the same people for decades. Here too he struck a chord. This is a thing that's being commonly questioned these days — whether it's Kaunda in Zambia or Tambo in the ANC or Motsuenyane in Nafcoc. There was a time when people revered existing leaders, but increasingly the feeling is that healthy organisations need fresh input.

In the end, sadly, nothing came out of the meeting. We left no wiser, still in doubt about whether to throw our weight behind Nation Building a la Klaaste and Mabe.

I and others were left with a sinking feeling of doubt about whether we blacks will ever get our act together. Will we always tear down everything that another person puts up? Will we always be paralysed by ideological conflicts, cursing us to quarrel over every initiative so that nothing happens?

My feeling is that Klaaste and Mabe did not have to wait around until somebody gave them a mandate. For that matter, who is in a position to give a mandate? They wanted to do something beneficial, and they stood up and did it. If some personal glory reflects upon them, that does not mean their effort must be denounced.

However, if I personally am to give active support to this Nation Building, I need to be satisfied on two counts. I need to know it will advance liberation, not merely create happier blacks for the white man to rule over, and I need a concrete idea of what it means.

The big thing coming up under Nation Building is a festive week consisting of things like a prayer meeting, a banquet, a music festival and a seminar for advertisers, and I do not see how these are building the nation. In any case, this festival is being organised by a white public-relations company and while I have nothing against white companies the fact is whites are already well built.

There are still queries in my mind, but I also query the motives of much of the opposition.

A diplomat recently came back from Lusaka and told me the word there is that Nation Building is a government ploy to woo people into government structures, which is a ridiculous thing to say. He was even told that Sam Mabe is a member of the Joint Management Committee. Nothing can be more ridiculous. It makes me wonder about other local initiatives branded heretical by Lusaka. Not everybody thinks the solutions lie beyond the Limpopo, and not all problems warrant safaris to Lusaka.

Even while Nation Building was being mauled in the Dube YWCA, another group was meeting at Ipelegeng Centre in White City, Jabavu. In theory, each meeting was for anybody. In practice, in the style of our times, the two meetings divided on ideological lines.

Just as everyone knew everyone at Dube, so that was the case at Ipelegeng. That is what black political meetings have become — great gatherings where the expected happens. No diverse thinking or fresh ideas are tossed about. The usual people speak, and the usual resolutions are taken.

The Dube meeting consisted of people with Africanist or black-consciousness leanings and people who were prepared to be seen with them. At Ipelegeng it was the opposite — the Charterists and ANC/MDM crew were there with their hangers-on.

That each meeting drew about equal numbers of "establishment" figures is another indication that the days of ANC/Charterist domination are numbered. Meanwhile, the so-called masses that everyone spoke about were not at either meeting and are about equally uninterested in both rival camps.

At Ipelegeng, as at Dube, the central topic was how to combat the return of lawlessness and collapse, but there, of course, *The Sowetan* endeavour was not even mentioned. I'm told most of the discussion consisted of complaints about the inactivity of the police — which while very correct and understandable is ironic coming from the people who a few years ago were doing their best to emasculate the police.

Soon afterwards, the Soweto establishment gathered yet again, for a plush breakfast meeting sponsored by *Tribute* magazine to discuss the role of the middle class in the liberation struggle.

It seems everyone agrees the struggle, which has always been in the name of the masses, has in fact been the property of the middle class all along. But there are few clear ideas as to whether this is natural or regrettable, and what it means. And to the voices asking for leadership and direction in restoring order to the townships, there were no answers.

While much has been written about the internecine war destroying lives in Pietermaritzburg, very little is being said about the hell-hole Soweto has again become after two years of respite.

Gruesome crimes are perpetrated in broad daylight and the law does not seem to be doing much about it. Today, in contrast to 1986, the collapse is not politically motivated but is rather a collapse into outright crime. It seems we are reaping the fruits of the era of ungovernability and the days of "liberation before education," because the criminals are predominantly teenagers.

In Naledi extension, a certain house belongs to a woman who is a live-in domestic servant in town. The house is left with her sons, who are into the car-stealing business. There is a bend in the road, where every motorist has to slow down almost to a stop. The boys and their pals lurk at the bend and pounce on the drivers, forcing them out of the car and taking it. Woe unto female passengers. This happens in broad daylight.

In Emndeni, there is a house where young thugs hold groups of several women prisoner. When they tire of the women, they go out and hunt for replacements.

There is also a new trend of kidnapping young girls, called jack-rolling. Nobody knows where the word originates, but girls who have been victims claim the jackrollers have slogans such as "jackrolling is not a crime, it is a game" and "it is not a rape, it is a game".

A teenager in Meadowlands thought she was smart and befriended boys in her area who were in the jackrolling game. One Sunday morning they pretended to be chatting her up and then shoved her into a car and drove off with her, taking her from one shebeen to another, while telling her what was going to happen to her when it was dark.

151

Come evening they stopped at a barren part of Tembisa, but what they had left out of their calculations was that by now they were so drunk she could escape. Far from home, she was given shelter by a kind family, who, however, had no way of contacting her frantic parents.

In Soweto, two particular cars — a BMW and a kombi — have become notorious for taking young girls by force. Many people in the township feel the police know what is going on but are not bothered about "black on black" crime — though the police say they apprehended a dozen alleged jackrollers early last month.

Now there are schools where students are organising vigilante gangs — a lot like 1986 but with different motives.

In Mofolo township, two teenagers were killed and a house set alight. It started on a Sunday afternoon when a girl of about 16 went to a shebeen in the company of boys (non-scholars). On their way, they met the girl's steady boyfriend who was a student. A fight ensued, and the student was shot dead.

That evening, his fellow students set alight the home of one of the boys. The next day, in full view of several people including her mother, the girl was beaten to death. Many people in Mofolo now fear that further repercussions are coming.

At Diepkloof Immaculata High School, students are fighting a virtual war with nearby gangs. It seems the students have set themselves up as guardians of morality, which is well intentioned but has quickly become a new abuse of power. Recently, one of the teachers, a married woman, was called out to discuss an urgent matter by a man with whom she serves on a welfare committee. She sat in the man's car outside the school, and when she returned the students told her she was of loose morals and not fit to teach them. Fearing assault, she resigned.

One of her male colleagues was locked out of the classroom when he intended to set the students a test. He too has resigned and so has another teacher, fearing pupils. Now parents are pleading with them to return, but there is no security for their lives.

At Fidelitas, also in Diepkloof, students locked teachers and the principal in a classroom. It's not clear what misdemeanor the teachers committed, but they were at the mercy of the students for hours and had to beg to be allowed to go to the toilet.

Amid all the talk of negotiations that will usher in a new South Africa, little is being done to address the realities of the townships. We have in our midst youngsters who have performed acts of heroism. Some have been maimed. There are those who survived detentions and came back to pick up the pieces of their lives and start anew.

But many have not been lucky. They have been tossed about by the storms. The schools would not have them back, their peers have moved to higher classes, and society shuns them.

What is left of a 15-year-old who hasn't been in a normal school set-up for five years? How does he fill the 24 hours of the day? What does he feel as he sees former schoolmates carrying on life as a normal activity and realises he's at a dead end?

We are in a Catch 22 situation. To expect the law alone to cope with this situation is to court even more violence. We need to put our energies together to reorient these youngsters and create normality and respect. We also need the press to bring out the real issues destroying the fabric of society, instead of skirting over them by paying attention only to the press statements of politicians. The problems need to be highlighted now, not ignored until they are out of hand as in 1976.